The Tower

A Parable of Relationships

The Tower, A Parable of Relationships, by Clay Watts

Cover design © 2015 by Ben Watts

ISBN 13: 978-1515384373
ISBN 10: 1515384373

Acknowledgments

To Adam, my son, who has also worked in towers, for his frank and perceptive comments.

To Ben, my son, for the cover design as well as for his thoughtful comments.

To Dominic Herbst, developer of the Restoring Relationships Model.

To Lori Janke, my editor, for her smooth phrasing and suggestions.

To Sarah Smith, writing as Precarious Yates, for her expertise in formatting and publishing.

To Kathy, "the wife of my youth," for her loving encouragement and wise suggestions.

Table of Contents

Introduction

When one of my sons read an early draft of this little book, he was puzzled about the genre and the target audience. Is it business, psychology, religion, or what? Is it intended for a Christian or secular readership? I have to admit that it is even hard for me to pin down. It is a parable, or a series of parables, in that it tells simple fictional stories to illustrate valuable principles. It is about business because it pulls from my experience in business systems analysis, process improvement consulting, and project management with a large corporation and with several large law firms. It is also about improving interpersonal relationships as I have experienced in a life-changing program developed by a Christian psychologist.

The unifying theme is that healthy interpersonal relationships are the foundation to releasing productivity and creativity in everyday business and personal life situations. Relationships deal with caring about others and communicating with others, but we can only be truly effective in our relationships when we, ourselves, are emotionally healthy.

This story uncovers not only the power of healthy relationships, but the process of getting there. It is told through the eyes of three different people who are profoundly impacted by the Owner of a tower as he commissions its building, empowers its occupants, and impacts the surrounding community.

Come with me on this business fantasy, and imagine how the world could be changed one tower, one community, and one person at a time.

The Tower

PART ONE – The Building

The Builder

I am the Builder. The Owner wants me to construct one of the largest and finest towers ever built. It must be beautiful and yet functional. It will be magnificent. My first task is to find a suitable location. Some who work in the Owner's organization will want to live near the tower, but many will not; therefore, it should be near transportation facilities and within walking distance of many services. It should have a natural setting that will give the occupants a sense of peacefulness. The site, as well as the tower itself, should express the personality of the Owner. He is a very powerful yet humble man. He has a large organization that he thinks of as an extended family, so he wants to create an environment that will encourage relationships to grow and new ones to form. But the main purpose of the tower is to provide an atmosphere of productivity and learning. Ideally, the site will complement the tower with a careful balance of open spaces and efficient work areas that foster meaningful communication free from distractions. This all sounds wonderful, but how can I accomplish these seemingly contradictory goals? I need expert counsel.

The Consultants

I bring in a renowned Site Consultant. She has performed site analysis and selection for several world-class towers. She wants to understand the Owner's strategic goals and my project requirements. As she gently probes for information regarding attitudes and preconceived ideas, she determines that we have conflicting internal objectives. She points out that I am more concerned with practical issues of cost, schedule, and risk avoidance, whereas the Owner is more concerned with the overall harmony of function and design. Other key members of our team likewise have competing, or at least inconsistent, goals. She recommends that we work on resolving our internal differences regarding the basic goals and direction of the project first, and then call her back in to help with the site selection. Since she is the expert, I take her advice. Obviously, I am concerned about the cost and schedule impact of this delay so early in the project; however, my desire to minimize risk prevails, so I bring in a Strategic Planning Consultant to help us develop goals and objectives that are consistent with the Owner's vision.

While the new Consultant is quite engaging, it is a slow and painful process. After several days of intense conversations, we finally realize the value of clarifying our direction. We are quite pleased when we come to an agreement on the general issues of why we are building the tower and how we should go about constructing it. For example, we discover that the Owner's view of nurturing relationships is a lot deeper and more complex than we thought. It is not just a matter of providing proximity and access among groups that work together, but he wants to encourage relationships to go below the surface and generate high levels of trust. Secondarily, he wants us to create opportunities for spontaneous interactions that can lead to new relationships and insights. Trust is critical for today's operations, but new insights will help ensure longevity of the organization. As another example, we explore the paradox of facilitating productivity while fostering creativity and continuous learning. We realize that the former results in efficiency, but the latter is needed for long-term effectiveness. This has many implications, the Consultant assures us, that will drive the design of the tower's interior space.

As the Strategic Planning Consultant helps us clarify our goals and objectives, we begin to understand that this process is not just helping us to locate, design, and build a tower. We immediately see how both the physical site and the building can help achieve the Owner's organizational vision. But even more importantly, we are deepening our understanding of why we are doing our jobs and how we can work more efficiently and effectively. This leads to many side conversations about improvement opportunities that have nothing to do with the tower. I have a fleeting thought that perhaps the Owner knew this would happen, and that the tower itself is not really the ultimate objective of this expensive and time-consuming project.

Ok, time to bring back the Site Consultant. She is obviously pleased with our progress and does not seem concerned with the time it took. She says her job will be much easier now. Within a few hours of reviewing our vision, goals, and objectives, she translates these into criteria for the location and characteristics of a building site. She brings in her team to identify potential sites and filter them down to the five most promising ones for our leadership team to evaluate. It is a difficult decision since there are so many factors and trade-offs to consider. With her help, we narrow the field to three locations and begin detailed inspections and evaluations of each.

At this point, our Marketing Director makes an offhand suggestion that will turn out to be of great importance. He simply says that perhaps we should visit not only with the local governments in each of the areas, but also with prominent architectural and city planning critics from the media. They are surprised at our invitation to participate in the evaluation process as independent observers, but they are not shy about providing input. They have remarkable insight on integrating the sites with the surrounding community with which they are intimately familiar. They even give us ideas on the building and landscape design, especially at the ground level.

The Architect

After several sessions with the Site Consultant, we eliminate one of the locations based on expected difficulties in working with the local governments, businesses, and community leaders. We decide to bring in our Architect to help with the final site selection from the two remaining candidates. The Architect warns us that this will increase his initial assessment and concept fee since he will have to develop two proposals that could be quite different. We have been learning, however, that it is better to take more time to explore alternatives and focus on what we really need before committing to the entire project.

Sure enough, the Architect consults with a colleague who was able to point out issues with one of the sites that would make the tower much more expensive and would limit the designs he could propose. The area has little-known geological anomalies that would require much larger and deeper piers given the footprint and height of the tower. So with little additional cost, the Architect keeps us from wasting a lot of time and money on site engineering. Instead, we ask the Architect to focus on the one remaining site as the Owner begins the land acquisition process.

Architects are interesting people. They are artistic and creative, yet practical and knowledgeable about everything from building codes to the characteristics of materials and the intricate details of construction. Our Architect is no exception. He relishes the challenge of integrating all aspects of the project. He is impressed that we have identified our vision, strategy, and objectives that are to be complemented by the tower. One example involves a small stream running through the property. The Architect would normally divert it to avoid interference with the tower and construction effort; however, with the Owner's emphasis on integrating form and function, he recommends preserving the natural flow of the stream and allowing it to dictate the ground level landscaping and foundation footprint. His architectural firm gives him a hard time over this eminently impractical and costly recommendation, but he recognizes the long term value of maintaining the site's natural and historical features. They nicely complement the Owner's goals, and send a message of consideration for the community that no amount of PR could convey.

The Space Designer

The Architect allows the site and the organization's goals to dictate other features and design concepts. One of the most difficult areas is facilitating the development and maintenance of personal relationships among the occupants. The Architect brings in a specialist to analyze the groups of people and how they interact. This allows areas to be designed to support how the employees function, and to place them in proximity based on the expected strengths of their interactions with one another. This is fairly easy to do on a floor with a combination of open spaces, private and semi-private offices, and flexible workstations; however, the degree of relationships and interactions envisioned by the Owner is much more extensive than the Architect has encountered in past assignments. He has to find a way to overcome the separation of floors from one another.

In another example of insight gained through seemingly random connections, the solution to the problem of separation comes from a fish aquarium. The Space Designer, sitting in a dentist's office, observes an aquarium and notices the freedom of the fish to move in all dimensions. He wishes he could design such a space for people inside tall buildings, if only there was some way to effortlessly swim like a fish, moving up and down as well as forward and backward. Up until this point, the only way vertical motion for people has been achieved is through stairs (requiring great physical effort), or escalators and elevators (which must be located sparingly due to their great cost and electro-mechanical requirements). What is needed is some buoyant force that is ubiquitous, easy to tap into, and requires only small, incremental energy expenditure, such as a personal elevator without the mechanical trappings.

The answer begins to materialize in his mind. The Space Designer envisions smaller versions of an elevator, using transparent tubes with magnetic propulsion that are distributed throughout a floor. One to three people could step into a small cylindrical pod that immediately rises or falls at the push of a button. Most "tubels" would extend through at least 3 floors, but some as many as 5 or 7 floors. Thus, people could be no more than a few seconds from the people above and below them. This extends the opportunities for enhancing relationships by at least a factor of 3. It also could reduce the number of traditional elevators.

Of course, the only problem with this idea is that "tubels" don't exist! But that doesn't deter the Space Designer. He convinces the Architect to reserve parts of a few floors where such devices could be installed at a later time, after the details of design and construction could be worked out. He further identifies several large groups that have occasional, but important, need for interaction, and positions them in three contiguous floors. The Architect then catches the creative spark and designs two experimental tubes spanning the three floors that are connected with an old-fashioned vertical conveyor loop belt with small platforms every 8 feet. An adventurous person could step on one of the platforms and be on the floor above or below in 10 seconds. Not very elegant, and a bit of a physical challenge, but it soon becomes the talk of the organization. Many group leaders lobby the space designer to assign the space to them. The demand is so great that the Architect provides several more "loopels" throughout the tower. The groups that would eventually occupy those floors begin to call themselves the "firemen" or the "miners," with double meanings referring to troubleshooters and analysts. An unexpected result of this old-fashioned innovation is that the groups find more reasons to visit one another, even before occupying the building, and their interactions provide many new ideas for products and process improvements.

The Creativity Effect

When others see that the Architect and Space Designer are able to implement what seems like a wild notion, other ideas begin to emerge. Groups like IT, Sales, and Product Design, who often work in project teams, ask for creative facilities that will enhance the ability of such teams to assemble on a moment's notice in a space that has all of the audio/visual, computer, and networking tools they need. One suggestion given is to create a menu of configurable displays made up of multiple touchscreens of various sizes. The Architect and Space Designer find cost-effective ways to implement these requests. They go even further by designing seating and work surfaces that are also easily reconfigured to accommodate the need for more people, or for more room to spread out papers and models. The assembly area furniture is custom developed to snap together like interlocking toys on the sides, but with legs that unfold from underneath as needed.

Once the creative juices of the Architect, Space Designer, and others begin to flow and are given liberty to influence the tower design, the floodgates of inspiration open. Many individuals and groups begin to consider new ways of doing their work and how the new space and facilities could help. They know that they have this one opportunity to affect their work environment, and they want to make the most of it. The atmosphere is so charged that even management catches the fever and begins to find ways to absorb and channel the creative energies. They actually take their people's suggestions seriously and work across departments to identify the best ideas and most cost effective ways to implement them. They present the building designers with a well thought-out list of desirable features, prioritizing them based on their perceived cost, difficulty of implementation, and contribution to the organization's vision and goals that had been established earlier. Of course, the managers do not know how or if these features could be incorporated, but they are pleasantly surprised when the designers accept many of the ideas. The designers are motivated to accommodate the requests, because they now see the importance of their design in helping the organization reach new levels of efficiency and effectiveness. The designers also love a challenge and want to show that they are no less creative, and that they can find even more cost effective or cost neutral ways to implement the requests.

The Exterior Design

The last stage of the tower design is the framework and exterior of the building. As if by magic, this develops out the organization's goals, the site selection, and the interior design. Retaining the site's natural contours means that the lower levels of the tower have to be very open. The ground floor becomes essentially a park, with the stream being expanded into several water features, and a series of paths, kiosks, and gardens. There is even a children's playground that becomes the most popular part of the property, used heavily by the in-house day care center. The other striking feature is the large atrium in the center that extends for several floors, giving the sensation of height, as well as allowing the interior of the lower floors to have a great view of the park. It is so attractive that the Architect places common eating and meeting areas around the atrium.

The biggest challenge becomes sunlight. The park area that is under the building would not get enough sunlight, even indirectly, to support plants and grass. Sparked by the other creative solutions for the interior design, the Architect engages a fiber optic lighting company to develop ways for outside light to be captured and transmitted to the atrium. The design not only allows the light to be diffused with a natural glow, but the placement of the collectors on the exterior of the building reduces the overall reflectivity of the structure.

The rest of the tower exterior design continues upward in a unique, organic spiral that complements the winding stream and paths of the park. The skin is composed of both flat and curved panes of a transparent material that can change translucence, absorb solar energy for supplemental power, and support exterior and interior automated window cleaning devices. Finally, the tower is topped off with a dramatic set of three spires that wind around one another to a single point.

The underlying theme throughout the design effort is cooperation and synergy among the various groups. Since all recognize that this is a spontaneous, bottom-up experience, they do not feel that they should push their particular agendas. They want the end result to be what is best for the organization. What really matters is that they are heard and that they are all cooperating for the common good.

The Construction Contractor

Now that the design is well underway – only the details are left to be worked out – it is time to get the construction bids. While I have several contractors in mind, I decide to apply some of the creative principles I have seen work so well during the design phase to the selection process of the contractors. My first criteria for developing a short list is to consider those who I know will be open to new ways of doing things and embracing innovative design concepts. Even more, I want someone who is not afraid to propose creative alternatives where a design concept may not be practical. Fortunately, I have worked with some of the best contractors in the country, so it is not difficult to come up with five names who meet these challenging criteria. I further narrow it down to three, based on whether the principal is available within the Owner's timeframe. Even if the contractor is the best, it is important to have his full attention and to not expect him to spread himself too thin.

Next, I engage the Strategic Planning Consultant again to evaluate the three contractors. She knows very little about construction, but she knows how to assess whether teams can work together effectively. She designs a simple exercise for each of the contractor management teams, also involving key players on my design team and the Owner's key executives on the project. First, the Owner's representatives prepare a document stating their organizational goals and objectives, revised to take into account what has been learned since the first such effort. Next, the design team prepares a set of drawings and high-level specifications representing the tower exterior and interior cross-sections. Finally, the Consultant provides both of these documents to the contractor teams and gives them two days to develop a rough bill of materials, construction schedule, and cost estimate. They understand that they will not be bound by any of this, but that it is just an exercise to see how they work together as a team. The Consultant mentions briefly that the other teams are available during the exercise, if needed, but she emphasizes the task objectives of the contractor team. However, the real point of the exercise is only partially to see how well the contractor team works together. The larger test is whether they will go beyond their own boundaries to reach out to the Owner's team and the design team, demonstrating that they see themselves as part of the larger effort. Nothing is said about how they should do this, or even if they should do so.

The contractor teams work their assignments on separate days to make sure that the Owner and design teams are available if called upon. Each of the contractor teams begins by reviewing the documents, estimating the materials and construction techniques needed, and feeding the information into sophisticated computer models. Two of the teams work all day to analyze and refine their plan, finding shortcuts and devising new techniques to accommodate the innovative designs while still meeting the Owner's cost objective. Knowing that they are being evaluated on their teamwork, they are careful to reach consensus at key points during the two-day exercise. One of the teams even assigns a person to assess periodically how they are working together and to suggest ways to improve.

The third team starts out like the other two, but after reviewing the documents, it runs into a snag. One of the construction executives, the Procurement Director, is very concerned about the tower skin materials and envisioned construction requirements. The rest of the team tries to convince him that it can be done as designed, and that the both the skin and the tower design concept are critical components in meeting the organizational objectives. The skin is unusual, but it supports the creative shape of the building, which in turn supports the Owner's primary goal of symbolizing an organic, interrelated organization through the tower structure. The Procurement Director is not convinced. His gut tells him the untried materials will not only be costly to fabricate and difficult to install, but he is particularly concerned about the possibility of extensive leaking in extreme weather conditions. He refuses to back down, even when confronted by the Managing Director's appeal to work together as a team.

Finally, the Procurement Director insists on a meeting with both the design team and the Owner's representatives. He presents the problem and asks if they will consider a "…less fluid exterior design in exchange for less fluid in the interior," as he wryly puts it. He also notes that a more conventional design would allow better use of the interior space and likely have a more positive psychological impact on the workers. Surprisingly, both the design and Owner's teams are receptive to the critique. It turns out that they also have reservations about the exterior design, but for different reasons. The Architect likes the flowing shape that is quite cutting edge, but is a bit surprised that the Owner's team didn't question the practicality of building it with all new, untried materials that would have to be developed and tested extensively. The Owner's team is so enthralled with the appearance of the tower that they assume the Architect wouldn't design something that was high risk. After seeing the Owner's team's enthusiastic, unchallenging response to the design, the Architect doesn't want to overstate the risks. In the end, both teams are actually relieved to be challenged and brought back to reality.

Together, the three teams quickly modify the design to closely resemble the original shape, but with more conventional materials and construction methods. From a distance, the tower would retain the overall impression of organic fluidity, but with a much more practical use of the space and the Owner's money, and at greatly reduced risk of future problems and cost overruns. Needless to say, the Owner selects the third contractor. With a small effort, they dodge a potential bullet and, even more importantly, are confident that other construction issues will be quickly raised and fairly dealt with for the benefit of the organization.

The Project Manager

Well, I have successfully completed the first major phase of the grand project. I have assembled a world-class team that is working together with expertise and integrity. We have identified and met the Owner's goals and objectives with an innovative design. Most of all, everyone involved is convinced that the tower embodies the vision of the Owner. It has already brought together disparate talents, and generated unprecedented creativity that is not only inspiring, but meets the functional needs of the entire organization. This is just an example of what the Owner desires for the organization as it works together to meet the needs of its customers and stockholders.

But now, as they say, everything degenerates into work. The best design is of no value if it can't be implemented, so my job begins in earnest. My first request of the building contractor is to name the Procurement Director as the Project Manager. There are protests all around, especially from the Procurement Director, but I prevail. At the request of the new Project Manager, I amend the budget to include a Deputy Project Manager who would be the contractor's choice for Project Manager. He is to be the communication channel with the rest of the contractor's team and subcontractors. All key decisions still have to be run by the Project Manager, and he is the point of contact with the design and Owner's teams. I trust him implicitly to look out for the Owner's interests and to raise issues that might be sensitive or even embarrassing to any party. This responsibility so freely given by the client weighs heavily on the ex-Procurement Director, but he is honored by the trust placed in him. He does everything he can to keep all players informed of the issues and risks.

With his procurement background, the Project Manager brings new perspectives to his role. He is able to draw parties together and negotiate agreements that are beneficial to both sides. He is an expert at managing contracts with the subcontractors, and he does not allow a penny to be wasted. While the schedule is important, his priority is delivery of a quality result. He is very careful to review the design specifications, questioning every detail, until there is full understanding of what is being delivered. His attention to the specifications results in faster construction because of fewer mistakes and rework. It also results in higher quality since compromise is not needed to compensate for the additional cost of miscommunication and lost productivity.

The Deputy Project Manager, far from being miffed at not having the top title, is relieved at being able to focus on the construction schedule and details. He does not have to deal with many of the client issues and meetings and feels more productive than ever. He is always available to the construction supervisors, who know that the Project Manager and the rest of the contractor management have complete confidence in his expertise. The Project Manager always defers to him on construction issues. If he has any reservations or questions, he allows the Deputy to privately explain his reasons before bringing another perspective. The two become friends and find that they have several common interests outside of work.

Cross-Functional Meetings

The Project Manager makes one other organizational decision that revolutionizes the worksite. From his procurement experience, he knows the value of getting a variety of inputs on product selection. The sales, design, engineering, and construction groups often have different perspectives. When he goes to the trouble to solicit all of their input on important procurement decisions, he always gets better results. So as a construction project manager, he takes the unprecedented step of bringing the various trades and subcontractors together twice a month to review the upcoming tasks. This is very uncomfortable for the Deputy Project Manager, who is used to dealing with each group separately so as not to get into arguments and jealousies about who is listening to whom. After a rocky start, the cross-functional meetings begin to shed light on important bottlenecks and potential delays that would not have been seen without interaction between the groups.

For example, the steelworkers' and concrete workers' jobs go hand in hand, but they rarely talk about how one affects the other. At one of the semi-monthly meetings, however, the steelworker supervisor makes a comment about how long it takes the concrete workers to tie the floor forms on to the steel beams. He says it would be easy to weld the tie-ons before they are hoisted in place so the forms could be set immediately. This way, they wouldn't have to wait for the welders to navigate the structure with all of their materials. The concrete supervisor recognizes the value of this idea and adds that, if they are welding the tie-ons on the ground, they could also cut the rebar and attach it to the appropriate beam before being hoisted up. Of course, this would require the steelworkers and concrete workers to work together on the beams, and the crane operator would have to adjust how he handles the beams due to the larger size and weight. Within hours, the supervisors make changes to the job orders, and the scheduler agrees to tweak the daily task list.

The Deputy Project Manager congratulates those involved in saving several days on the overall schedule, and making the job smoother and safer for all. As word spreads to the workers of the changes, rather than complaining about changing the way they have always done it, they are already seeing the benefits of cooperating and being open to new ideas. This is becoming the norm, and they actually congratulate their supervisors on making their jobs easier and doing the right thing to improve the building process. A couple of workers even mention aloud that they, too, will be looking for opportunities to suggest improvements.

The Deputy Project Manager, who had resisted the idea of the semi-monthly meetings as a waste of time initially, is now the biggest supporter. He enthusiastically notifies the supervisors of the issues he is facing several days before each meeting and asks for their help. They, in turn, mention the issues to their workers at the daily safety briefing, and ideas are tossed back and forth throughout the day. By the meeting, each supervisor typically has at least one idea or question for another group to solve. The Deputy Project Manager says he has never seen anything like it in his many years of managing building projects. He finds that the more he compliments and encourages his supervisors, the harder they work to improve the cooperation and atmosphere of the job site.

As he sees the Deputy begin to take hold of the new process, the Project Manager wisely chooses not to attend the semi-monthly meetings. He knows that the Deputy will have even greater ownership, and will have better ideas of his own, if the Project Manager isn't looking over his shoulder. The Project Manager further illustrates his confidence in the Deputy by bringing him to the monthly Owner's meeting to report on the building progress, and in particular, to report on the issues and resolutions that have been developed. It is an opportunity for the Deputy to shine, and to fully recognize the value of his teams' contributions. The Owner, himself, often attends these meetings, and at one point is so impressed with a creative solution described by the Deputy that he invites the Deputy Project Manager and the supervisors and the families of the two construction teams involved to be his guests at his skybox for that weekend's ball game. The entire site is buzzing all day at the news. The Deputy Project Manager later recognizes that there was a marked improvement in the construction schedule that could be traced to that one action by the Owner.

The Crisis

As the tower framework reaches the halfway point, a minor crisis occurs. I discover that one of the welding subcontractors is using an unlicensed welder on the floor beams. The original welder contracted a virus that took him off work for two months, but the hastily hired replacement lied about his license that had expired two years ago. When a worker from another subcontractor complains that the welder had been let go from a site they had both worked on a couple of years ago, it comes to the Deputy Project Manager's attention, and he carefully investigates the situation. He finds that the welder had been fired for drinking on the job. The welder could not find work for some time and, therefore, was not able to afford the fees to renew his license. He claims to have been sober since the firing, but he admits that his license has expired.

Of course, he has to be let go again, but the Deputy encourages him to do whatever it takes to renew his license. He promises the welder that he will not relay the news to other building firms so that he would have a chance to get work in the future. The Deputy then hires an inspector to test all of the man's welds and certify them in writing. The subcontractor gladly pays for the inspections, the tear-outs, and the rework needed to gain access to some of the welds. It turns out that the welder has done beautiful work, but he costs the subcontractor most of his profit, and the project several days of delay.

When the Project Manager finds out what has been done, he

is furious that the subcontractor has been let off so easily and that the welder has not been blackballed from the local construction sites. The Project Manager is a stickler for adhering to the letter of contracts, and as a career procurement director, always holds his vendors' feet to the fire if they violate any terms or even informal commitments. He is surprised that the Deputy, an experienced construction manager, is so lenient. Even more disturbing is the fact that the Deputy has not thought the incident important enough to bring to his attention until after the decisions were made. He confronts the Deputy in a meeting with the Owner and his management team to make sure they know about the issue. While the Project Manager does not have anything personal against the Deputy, he simply feels this is a serious breach of discipline that needs to be exposed.

After he finishes recounting the incident, the actions taken by the Deputy, and the consequences to the project schedule, the Project Manager looks expectantly at the Owner. The Owner pauses and quietly asks the Deputy why he did it. The Deputy explains that he had once been in a similar situation where he made a serious mistake, but that his supervisor had been lenient. He never forgot the favor, and had vowed that as long as the person involved was sorry for what he had done and promised not to do it again, that he would likewise be lenient to others. The Project Manager is shocked at the simplicity and naivety of the Deputy. He waits breathlessly for the Owner to take him apart. The Owner is silent for what seems like a full minute. He gazes at the Deputy, and then finally back at the Project Manager, and then the Owner speaks these words: "You know, that happened to me once, and it wasn't even my fault. A member of my crew made a serious mistake, but I knew he and his young family couldn't afford to miss a paycheck, so I took the blame and was dismissed. That was a long time ago, but I never regretted the decision. I have found that a little leniency at critical times will make a big impression on people, and will ultimately make them stronger."

The Deputy Project Manager never loses eye contact with the Owner as he says quietly, "Sir, I have looked forward to this moment for years. I was the young man on your crew who made that mistake. Your mercy was not in vain. I have dedicated my life to becoming the best construction worker, and then supervisor and manager that I could be. I have looked for every opportunity to forgive those who make a mistake, and then watch them redouble their efforts when they are given a second chance. I have likewise found that even if they have to take some consequences for their mistake, they are forever grateful and often become the most loyal and competent workers."

The entire room is quiet for another thirty seconds. Finally, the Project Manager speaks. He apologizes for being a bit testy about the incident and for wasting the time of the group. He is obviously moved by the interchange between the Owner and the Deputy, but he doesn't know what else to say at this very awkward moment.

The Building Skin and Interior Design

The rest of the steel skeleton and flooring goes up without incident. The decision to simplify the shape of the exterior makes the fabrication and installation much quicker. It is still quite dramatic-looking, even with the conventional materials and assembly techniques. The skin is another matter. The window panes are now simple, flat, rectangular panels with just a few standard sizes to facilitate assembly on the construction site; however, they are composed of a costly carbon-infused polymer that is stronger and lighter than glass. They also have small connectors in the edges to transmit power generated by the amorphous solar cells embedded in the panes. This award-winning innovation greatly reduces the reflectivity and power profile of the tower.

The skin design, however, poses problems during construction. The edges have to be precisely fitted into special aluminum frames that act as the wiring system to gather the solar power from the tower skin. The frames also have connectors to match up with the polymer panes and the adjacent frames. The skin assembly workers are given extensive training on aligning and inserting the panes and frames, spot welding them onto the tower skeleton, and testing them as they are put in place. While they are designed to be replaced from the inside of the tower, this requires great care during assembly to preserve a clean appearance for all joints and seams. A special caulking process is developed to enhance the durability of the seal, while allowing it to be easily refreshed and repaired in the future.

The new skin also requires a revolutionary approach to the materials and assembly of the interior space. In order to facilitate access to the skin and its power connectors from the inside, traditional drywall and window treatments cannot be used. Instead, the outside walls of the interior leverage the capabilities of the polymer panes to adjust reflectivity and translucence. Each interior space has controls to change one or more panes so that blinds are not needed. This allows the exterior office "walls" to be made with translucent plastic studs to which pictures, free-standing workspaces, and other pieces of furniture can be attached with pre-formed anchor holes. The whole effect is of floor-to-ceiling windows with variable translucence to create a sense of privacy or openness as desired.

The Interior Designer is initially challenged by the extensive exposure to the outside and use of clear studs, but she quickly adapts and convinces the Architect to even further reduce the use of drywall or plate glass for conference rooms and public areas. Instead, she experiments with fabrics and textured foam boards that can be arranged on the studs. The ceiling and floor grids have covered holes into which the studs can be inserted. The result is that they are easily moveable and can be used to change the size and shape of most meeting areas and offices. Likewise, power and cable outlets are available throughout the ceiling and floor grids.

The Mid-Project Critique

As the interior begins to take shape with the highly adaptable design features, I, the Builder, am beginning to understand that this is not a normal construction project. It started as an ambitious effort to build an iconic yet functional tower to support the Owner's goals and objectives for his organization. But now it has taken on a life of its own. Any one of the innovations, that seem to have come so easily, would have been a big deal at any of my other projects. To see so many unique ideas being proposed, accepted, and implemented – well, it has been surreal. And yet I do not have a sense that we are overextending ourselves or taking an unusual risk. It is just that we do not have any fear or anxiety about these innovations. It seems the most natural thing in the world to want to try new ideas and not be satisfied with the way things have always been done. Looking back at this point, I am trying to figure out how this has happened. I certainly did not initiate it, nor in any way did I expect something like this to happen. But why has it happened? Why does everyone involved in this project feel so good about it? Why are we working together so well and overcoming problems so easily? I decide to call the core team together to discuss these questions. I don't want to lose the opportunity to gain insight as to how we can replicate this on future projects.

I am a bit intimidated, and almost embarrassed, to state the purpose of the meeting the next day. I didn't tell the group what it was about, because I am not sure how it is going to go. So I start by saying that I would like the group to conduct a mid-project critique. Then I ask the standard questions: first, what has gone right with the project, and second, in what areas could we improve? The Project Manager is the first to speak. He says that he has never seen a project where the teams have worked so well together. I ask him and the others what they think has caused that. After a few seconds of silence, one of the Owner's reps finally clears her throat and says that she thinks it started when I brought the Strategic Planning Consultant in to make sure we all were on the same page regarding our goals and objectives. The Architect agrees, and adds that this unusual step inspired him to take a chance in developing the unique site and tower exterior concepts. He would never have been so bold if he had not known that he was supporting the Owner's vision of a highly relational and transparent organization. He was able to get buy-in from the others for the same reason – they all saw that it perfectly complemented the purpose and style of the organization.

The Deputy Project Manager jumps in with the comment that he agrees, but thinks it goes even deeper. While he came onto the project after the goals and objectives had been worked out, he is greatly impressed by the earnest desire of the Owner to build and support relationships among the employees, as well as with their customers and the surrounding community. It is clearly not just an afterthought to make everyone feel good, but rather a conviction that permeates every meeting that he observes. He sees it being worked out in daily, personal interactions as the difficult issues of a complex construction project arise. The Owner's reps set the tone in every situation. They show with words and actions that they value the thoughts and feelings of the people involved. The Deputy says he has never seen such real compassion, and even love, being shown in the messy details of life. This isn't the gushing attitude of touchy-feely types, but real people dealing with real problems, showing respect and concern for one another. He never hears people talking about others when they are out of the room. The whole atmosphere is catching. He finds himself taking on the same attitude of wanting to encourage and help his own construction teams.

Finally, another one of the Owner reps says that he, likewise, has been impressed from the beginning of the project with the devotion each person brings to the effort. He also thinks it is a reflection of the devotion that the Owner himself shows not only toward the project, but also toward each of his people and the consultants and contractors being brought on. He says that he is fairly new to the Owner's organization, and he is not just quoting the party line. He has been in several other respected, highly successful organizations previously, and this is simply not like any other. He can't explain it, but it just works. In fact, it seems to go against every other principle of leadership he has been taught. Sure, there is the same emphasis on productivity, efficiency, and cost/benefit awareness, but it is made abundantly clear that people and relationships are taken into account in every decision.

One example he gives is how the restaurants located around the atrium function. While the Owner wants them to be profitable and serve high-quality food, he also insists that each one creates an environment that will encourage the employees, other tenants, and visitors to the tower to freely interact with one another. He feels that the meal time is one of the most important opportunities to develop and deepen relationships. While he does not try to dictate how the restaurants achieve this goal, he asks them to include this value in their proposals. Everyone is surprised at the creativity shown by the restaurants, especially the chains. For example, with little additional expense, one restaurant is able to modify its traditional seating patterns to allow groups of different sizes to quickly change the table and chair configuration. Another one provides several partitioned areas to encourage customers to hold working sessions over lunch. Yet another provides an area designated for community tables where customers are encouraged to sit with others they don't know.

In the spirit of conducting a balanced critique, I next ask for areas that can be improved. One of the construction supervisors says that he has never seen it done before, but since this project is breaking new ground, he asks if we could bring on a night crew to perform some of the interior work that can be easily picked up by alternating teams. He suggests trying this approach, for example, on installing insulation and laying floor tile. The Deputy Project Manager says that he doesn't see why they shouldn't try that, at least on a pilot basis. He is then careful to affirm the supervisor's willingness to be creative in looking for ways to improve the schedule.

I look around the room to see if anyone else has something to contribute to the critique session. It has been an uplifting experience, one that I knew would end that way, but that surprised me nevertheless. I am amazed at how compassion for others and creativity seem to go hand in hand. You would think the opposite, that encouraging relationships and respect would be mawkish. But it seems that when people feel valued, they are free from fears and other constraints that weigh them down.

The Inspection Incident

After the meeting, one of the architects asks to speak to me privately. When we are in a nearby conference room, he confides that he has come across a disturbing piece of information. He was performing an as-built check on the refrigeration system. While he didn't design the system, he was checking the structure containing the system to insure that it met specs. He noticed that the pressure fittings are showing signs of stress, and it is not an isolated incident; he found that over a third of the fittings need further inspection and testing. I thank him for being observant, and contact the Plumbing Inspector. I ask him to come in first thing the next day to re-inspect the fittings.

When the Plumbing Inspector arrives, I sense a defensive attitude right away. He is indignant that I am questioning his previous inspection results, and all but refuses to perform another more detailed inspection using a time-consuming pressure test. I show him the indications that the architect found. He is even more indignant when he finds that it is a junior architect who is questioning the fittings. I finally recognize that he is stalling and is not going to do the inspections as I am requesting. I tell him that I will contact his supervisor if he won't do it. He says fine, and that he doesn't have time to spend on it today anyway. He is already late for his first appointment at another job site.

As soon as he is gone, I make the call, not to his immediate supervisor, but to the Co-owner of the plumbing inspection agency, whom I happen to know from a large job a few years ago. I am suspicious of the inspector's reaction and decide to go to the top to see what is really going on. I know that the agency has grown dramatically in the past few years, and I have an odd feeling that they may have brought on people who do not have the adequate training or experience needed for this highly skilled job. As I catch up with the Co-owner about his company and its surprising growth, I let him know about the current problem. He pauses for an uncomfortable length of time and asks if we can meet at a restaurant across town tomorrow after he has time to look at the records and talk to the supervisor. I feel that my concerns are more real than I had imagined.

Sure enough, when we meet the next afternoon, the Co-owner's face is stern. He starts by apologizing for the inspector's attitude, and sets up a time for two very experienced inspectors to perform the extensive testing I am requesting. He then lets me know that he has fired the inspector, confirming my fears that something was wrong with the whole plumbing operation. The Co-owner explains that this is the third incident in as many years with this inspector, and the second time with the same plumbing contractor. After some quick but thorough detective work, the Co-owner had determined that the inspector and his supervisor were taking bribes from this, and perhaps other, plumbing contractors to shortcut their inspections to save time and money for the contractor. He had apparently been unusually sloppy on this job, not performing any inspections, and even falsifying documents to say that he had done them. When he and the supervisor denied any wrongdoing, the Co-owner showed them the conclusive evidence and told them to leave immediately. They were furious and threatened a lawsuit; however, the Co-owner is confident that they will not only not get a lawyer, but will probably try to leave town since their reputation will not allow them to find work locally. The Co-owner says that he, in fact, plans to bring suit against them to recover the cost of the rework and to make sure they will not do the same to other builders throughout the state.

Of course, I report this incident the next day to the Owner, half expecting him to ask for mercy for the two inspectors. However, I am somewhat shocked that not only is he not the least bit merciful, but he immediately calls the inspection agency Co-owner to let him know how disappointed he is, and to ask that he join the suit against the two men. He is not interested in suing the agency, but he wants to make sure the men are fully punished for their misdoings. When he gets off the phone, I stare at him with what must have been a puzzled expression. He knows exactly what I am thinking, and without a pause, says that there is a time for mercy and there is a time for justice. Then he returns my stare, turns, and walks quietly away.

The Grand Opening

The tower construction has progressed on schedule, and even a little under budget. I am pleased to see how the innovations in the interior have been installed without problems, and how the furnishings and fixtures are working out so well. My inspectors are finding very little to include on their punch lists, and I am eager for the Owner's representatives to begin their final walkthroughs. As the finishing touches are added, the walkthroughs begin. I have never seen such thorough inspections. Every inspector has a tablet with 3D views of the entire tower. They touch an area to record their observations and code the priority of the modification or repair needed. Most of the items are cosmetic, but there are a few unfinished items and equipment or furnishings that don't quite work as expected. Even these experienced inspectors are surprised at the relative lack of significant discrepancies, especially given the unusual designs and materials being used. The punch lists are electronically delivered to the appropriate subcontractors who quickly address them in a matter of days.

Finally, the big day arrives – the grand opening of the finest tower in the world, at least in my opinion. There may be a few that are taller or with more square footage, but none with the overall beauty of design, the integration of form and function, and the many innovative features. Most of all, however, this tower facilitates and embodies the purpose of the organization and of its visionary Owner. Everyone eagerly awaits the Owner's address to the employees, the builders, and the community representatives. A hush falls over the boisterous crowd as he take the temporary stage on the ground floor, surrounded by the futuristic escalators, water features, playground, and natural landscaping. Without raising his voice, he commends the visionaries who conceived, designed, and built the tower, in spite of all the skeptics that derided each innovation and non-traditional component. He begins to recount the more daring innovations, such as the natural contours and openness of the ground level, the organic shape and energy-efficient exterior skin, and the flexible interior that allows teams to work together in new and highly effective ways. He even pokes a little fun at the groups that are already making plans to use the unusual loopels, referring to their daring use of 19th century technology. His point is not lost, however, that even old concepts can be adapted in new ways to create exciting opportunities.

He then focuses on the organization's purpose and how it is reflected, facilitated, and ultimately enhanced by the inanimate tower. He explains how the design elements intentionally improve opportunities of the employees to meet spontaneously, and how this encourages them to seek out ad hoc relationships that can lead to new friendships, interdepartmental alliances, and yes, new ways to improve their products and serve their customers better. He challenges and authorizes every employee to visit with one another, regardless of rank, experience, or area of expertise. He confides that his best and most profitable ideas come from chance encounters with people whose perspectives and experiences are totally different from his own.

He then admonishes the administrative and support groups to

be especially bold in approaching the people they serve, to find out both what they really need and what they don't need, such as red tape and unnecessary rules. After some of the other groups applaud this, he turns to them and challenges them to, likewise, spend time with their customers to listen to their needs. He stops, raises his voice, and says, "I mean really, really listen to them. Not just their spoken needs, but their feelings that indicate their true needs. Just as you want the admin staff to truly understand that you need the tools to do your job better, make sure you in turn truly understand what tools you can provide your customer. This only works if you thoroughly understand what he really needs to do his job better. Perhaps deep down he is fearful about trying our product because it will require a new process. Perhaps he loves the product but is under pressure to cut his budget and has no idea how to justify something that will only cost more in the current year, even though it saves money over the next two years."

"Listen, listen, listen," the Owner continues. "Then reach down in your innermost being and ignore the impulse to give the standard response. Instead, put yourself in his place and imagine what you would like to hear in that situation. What would meet your real, unspoken need? That's what the designers of this tower did. They created the opportunity to listen to us. They looked at the big picture as we presented it, not as they were expecting to hear it. Just like them, you be bold enough to do something new and uncomfortable. Take a chance and address that real need, even if it's not what would seem to meet your immediate objectives."

The Builder's Next Job

As the Owner winds down his celebratory speech, I begin to think about my next job. The tower has gained so much notoriety that I have my choice of several attractive assignments. After working with the Owner and his team, however, I decide that money and reputation are no longer as important as I once thought. I choose to take a job building an orphanage in a major city in East Africa. It is to be a showcase for the President of the country to demonstrate his support for the orphans of AIDS victims.

The thing that attracted me to the project was the desire of the President to use the building itself to symbolize the concern for disadvantaged children. It was to be a beacon that would draw other countries and NGOs to embrace the President's dream of building such orphanages and other care facilities all over the continent. I couldn't resist the opportunity, not just to do something worthwhile, but also to be given the liberty to create something beautiful, yet functional. I know something the President doesn't know. I know how to make this more than just a building and a symbol. I know how to take one man's vision and show how it can inspire a group of people, an entire community, and perhaps even a nation. I know how to bring together the creative energies of many teams to develop, not just an innovative design and building, but a spirit of cooperation and caring that will saturate those who are to work in, and interact with, the building. Yes, I will make a new thing.

PART TWO – The Employees

The HR VP

I am the Human Resources Vice President. I report to the Owner, and have been directly involved in the design and construction of the tower from the beginning. The Owner trusts me to represent the interests of the employees, as I have done for him in many other locations. The tower, however, is his crowning achievement. It is a fitting complement to the consolidation of his widespread organization into one location. My job is to make sure this coming together of disparate functions yields overall benefits to our customers, employees, and stockholders. I realize this is a complex task, since each of the separate entities has developed its own culture and ways of doing things.

Of course, our stockholders and employees both think that this means cost cutting through elimination of duplicate staff functions and consolidation of products and services. I have learned over the years, however, that cost cutting is a short-sighted strategy that often leads to poorer service and lower quality products for the customers. I plan to look for synergies to expand the scope of the organization, although that will be a major challenge. The toughest part, however, is overcoming the cultures of the different locations and functions. People don't change their habits and ways of thinking easily. And if they are forced to do so, they spend more time being defensive and frustrated than they spend finding better ways to serve the customer.

I have been a careful observer, as well as participant, in the building of the tower. I, like the others involved, have been in awe at the creativity, practical innovation, and teamwork that have produced such a beautiful, yet functional, building. More than anything else the Owner has accomplished, the tower has been a picture of not just how to run a complex project, but how to bring people together to be efficient and effective by releasing their creative energies. Creativity is the catalyst for productive change that overcomes the inherent inertia in any organization. It is this creativity that will be the foundation for our success.

Relationships Emphasis

The surprising thing about the tower project has been the emphasis on relationships. It was a primary objective stated at the outset, and it drove the design in many ways. Since it was talked about so much, the people involved in the project began to believe it. And even before the employees moved into the tower, the emphasis on relationships influenced the way they interacted with one another.

Even more than simply talking about valuing relationships, the employees were able to see that the Owner's team was taking it seriously. Decisions were made, and money was being spent in tangible ways, to encourage the formation of new relationships, as well as to enhance existing relationships. That sent a powerful message that this was an intentional and well thought-out effort. While there have been skeptics, most knew that the Owner had very good reasons for making relationships central to his organization's vision and purpose. Now it is up to me to see that the relationships goal, and other goals stated by the Owner, are implemented.

First, I recognize that all employees think they are relationship experts. Don't they deal with relationships all day, every day? That is, of course, like believing that everyone is an expert on grammar and syntax because they talk a lot every day. We may not even remember the basics of grammar and standard usage that we learned in junior high school, or if we do remember vaguely, we don't necessarily choose to regard, much less follow them. How many people these days say things like, "Thanks for inviting my husband and I to dinner," instead of "Thanks for inviting my husband and me to dinner"?

It's the same with relationships. There are a lot of written and unwritten rules, guidelines, and local preferences, many of which are counterproductive. As the HR officer, I know how to promulgate, train, and enforce the written rules, e.g., through a policy on sexual harassment. Even with all my efforts, I know that the letter, and certainly the spirit, of that policy are often violated knowingly and intentionally. But I have no idea how to inculcate this guideline, or any other policy that governs interpersonal relationships, into the thinking and behavior of the employees. I do know that the best examples of people following the intent of such policies are found in areas where the leader is both committed to them and demonstrates them in daily words and actions. For example, when a female department head dresses modestly but attractively, uses polite language, and shows respect for men and women equally, she sends an unambiguous message that even sexual innuendo, much less harassment, will not be tolerated.

The relationships that the Owner has in mind, however, go far beyond legality-oriented HR policies. He is certainly concerned about people, their well-being and job satisfaction, but he is even more interested in their feelings and aspirations. It is in these areas that creativity is either engendered or hindered. A person can be relatively healthy and happy with her work, but if she is consumed with worry about the influence her teenage son's friends are having on him, she is not likely to go much beyond fulfilling the basics of her job duties. Or a salesman may be making good money, but if his wife is threatening divorce, he is not likely to be really listening to the customer across the desk from him. Or a new employee may have great ambitions to be a leader in his department, but if his supervisor keeps putting him down so he will not be a threat, the young man may become sullen and non-productive, or he might simply leave.

Organizational Change and the Value of Relationships

The Owner tells me that, with the new tower and all of its

features that encourage relationships and teamwork, I should focus on issues regarding the consolidation of disparate parts of the organization. He keeps reminding me that we have a great opportunity to set the tone, from the top down, to value positive relationships in the midst of the busyness and stress of everyday activities. He has given me free rein to work with the top executives, one-on-one and in small groups, to learn how to do this and to practice it in real ways. I have developed a plan to take a first step and just reviewed it with him. He really likes the approach, and asks me to give it a try at a special meeting of his staff.

As the executives file in the conference room a week later, I touch a couple of buttons on my phone to start some quiet music playing. I get looks from a couple of them, but most keep on chatting about the issues they are having. When the last person sits down, I touch another button on a map of the room to darken the front area, where part of the wall comes alive with a short video. In the background is the same music that I played as they were coming in. The video is about a large, extended family sitting around the dinner table, discussing various topics in groups of two or three. Finally, the grandfather, whose house it is, clears his throat as he picks up on a conversation between two of his sons. They were discussing a recent investment opportunity they had researched together. They had decided that they would each put in a significant amount of their savings, hoping to generate a new stream of income outside of their normal portfolios and day jobs. The outcome would depend on the skills and resourcefulness of a man, whom they both know fairly well, who was soliciting investors to support his new business. The brothers were excitedly talking about the latest equipment the entrepreneur installed and how it will enhance the business's volumes and profit margin.

Their father interrupts politely with a simple question. He asks how the newly hired employees of this business venture are doing. The older brother looks puzzled, and says that he isn't sure. He knows they have been working long hours, but everyone seemed to be focused on getting the business up and running when he and his brother visited the shop recently. The younger brother nods, and agrees that they all seemed very determined to make the new venture work. He says that the employees were focused and busy to the point that they were not even aware of the visitors.

The younger brother then shares that he saw one incident where an operator was getting frustrated with his supervisor about a procedure that didn't make sense to him. When the operator tried to tell the supervisor how he had handled similar situations at his previous job, the supervisor tensed his face, rolled his eyes, and said, "Well, we are not that company. Just do as I am telling you." He then turned around and walked off shaking his head from side to side.

The brother pauses, and says that he did notice a couple of other employees who seemed to be tense and even agitated when asked a question by a fellow employee. But he was only there for a few minutes and didn't really get to talk to anyone besides the person guiding them through the facility. Their friend, the new owner, explained these incidents off-handedly as growing pains and the fact that everyone is working long hours.

The father clears his throat again and says that if the employees are under a lot of stress, he hopes they have times when they can be with their families and recharge. He adds that it would be a shame if they succeed in getting the business off to a good start, but burn out in the process. The brothers glance at each other with puzzled expressions. Later, as they are drying and putting up pans from dinner, they discuss their father's comment. Since the venture is an investment to them, the more important question is whether it is on track to grow and make money – isn't it? No pain, no gain, you know.

As I turn off the video screen and bring the lights up, I pause for a few seconds to allow the room to contemplate the clip they have just seen. Then I ask for comments. The Sales VP is the first to speak up. He has just been given global responsibility for sales for the largest consumer products division, and can obviously identify with the entrepreneur starting up a new venture. He and his team are working crazy hours to bring the various sales groups together to develop the processes and incentives for the new organizational alignments. He has also taken upon himself the cross-departmental goal of providing feedback to product development and engineering. This feedback will enhance profitability by streamlining the product lines, while still accommodating the needs of the distinctive market segments that his team is working nights and weekends to define. It is a monumental task, and he has been feeling the pressure for months. He considers himself a team player, and after learning the lessons of the tower construction and organizational consolidation, he feels that he is leading the charge to find synergy by developing new relationships across the organization.

As he speaks, I can hear the weariness in his voice. He tries to overcome it with his usual high energy and fast pace. He says he doesn't see the point of the clip. He is very self-aware and assumes the others in the room see the comparison with his group's recent high-stress activities. He continues by justifying the entrepreneur's actions, saying that personal sacrifices must be made any time you want to start up a new work that involves a lot of change. There will be tension and stress, but that is just part of the job, and it can motivate people to work harder and focus on the core issues and deadlines. Everyone knows, he reminds the room, that if you want something done, you give it to a busy person.

He sits down, and the room is silent for a few seconds. Slowly the VP of Product Development rises and speaks in his low voice with deliberate pauses for emphasis. He commends the Sales VP for both taking the initiative to rethink the product line and for reaching out to the product development group to coordinate the effort. This would never have happened in the previous culture, and it has created excitement in his team as well. "However," he continues after a long pause, "my team is likewise becoming stressed, and I am seeing the signs of unusual tension, as in the video clip. The organizational consolidation itself is a second full-time job for my team and me. I was hoping to put off the product streamlining and re-evaluation until after the organizational changes were in place. I realize that there can be interactions between the two efforts, but it is a huge task to take on all at one time. I have not wanted to dampen the enthusiasm of the sales team to look at product changes, but if we are supposed to be honest in this meeting, I have to say that it's killing my group to try to take that on now. It's a great idea, and much needed, but the timing is not good for us. We are even beginning to see serious lapses in our normal responsibilities due to being stretched too thin."

Uncharacteristically, the Sales VP hardly knows what to say. He addresses no one in particular, and says that he is just trying to do the right thing. He reminds the group that the Owner is sending a clear message that this new building is to a represent a new era for cooperation among groups, for new levels of creativity, and for developing stronger relationships in general.

I am reading body language in the group and sense that most are sympathetic with one of the two views being expressed. I commend the two executives for pinpointing the exact issue the video clip was intended to highlight. I tell them that the Owner has concerns about this, and wants me to address it with the executive team. I then summarize the issue raised by the two executives, and ask those in the room to break into small groups of 4 or 5. Their task is to restate the issue in their own terms, to discuss if the issue is relevant for their work teams, and if so, to explore what practical guidelines might be put in place to resolve it. I quickly segment the room into quadrants and ask them to move the tables and chairs to form discussion groups. I give them 30 minutes to come up with both a re-statement of the issue that includes anything else they may see, and the top two actions that could help resolve it. I intentionally separate the VPs of Sales and Product Development so that they are not put on the spot in their groups, and so that they can hear other perspectives.

I am grateful that the tower designers provided variable white noise levels for the meeting areas, and I take advantage of that as I crank up the volume to allow the groups to have a spirited discussion without being distracted by the others. I move around from table to table and am surprised at the depth of feeling being expressed by several of the executives. The Owner had been right in calling out this particular issue as critical for managing large-scale change. The discussions are still going strong after 30 minutes, so I give them another 10 minutes and ask them to begin zeroing in on their top two solutions. The space designers had thoughtfully provided a hidden clock display in each meeting area, so I use my smartphone app to reveal it and set it on timer mode. As the time winds down, I turn the white noise back to the minimum level and ask the groups to stay where they are, but turn toward the front of the room.

Without me saying a word, the group with the Sales VP asks to be the first to speak. The Accounting Director is almost excited when he stands to speak on behalf of the group. He acknowledges the issue is essentially what I stated 40 minutes ago, with one addition. Their group sees that the way each executive interprets and expresses the goal of improving relationships could be another factor. For example, the Sales

VP sees it as meaning cross-departmental relationships. This implies working together to ensure that all departments have input into decisions and end-to-end processes that affect them. Critical communication like this is often not requested, or even thought about, so the Sales VP feels he is going above and beyond to take advantage of the organizational changes to provide fresh ideas on a process that his team has to live with.

However, others at the table recognize the impact the magnitude of the effort will have on relationships within each department when each person has to do their normal job, as well as juggle complex projects with short deadlines. While that may be exciting for a few, it stresses everyone else beyond their ability to be thoughtful and considerate of one another. Thus, interpersonal relationships suffer greatly. The stress often affects the employee's relationships at home, which in turn diminishes their effectiveness at work. Managers are working on these projects, delegating much of the work to their supervisors, and the supervisors are then distracted from keeping their people productive and dealing with operational problems.

"But," the Accounting Director says with a smile, "we also discussed a couple of solutions to this dilemma, one short term and the other longer term. In the short run, we feel that managers and directors should protect their people from unnecessary stress due to organization-wide and interdepartmental issues. It is natural to take direction from the executives without questioning them about the bigger picture. When managers get a request to implement a new process or policy, they often read into that request that it is of the highest priority, and that it is their job to figure out how to do it with the existing resources in the timeframe given to them. I am sure we all agree that, often as executives, we are not aware of how much effort and cost some of our good ideas are going to consume. We implicitly depend on our managers to push back if they can't realistically handle a last-minute project. They just don't do that very often. They see it as not being a team player, or that it will indicate a lack of the drive, or creativity, to get it done. Most of us, however, don't really think through the ramifications of the top-down request, especially when it comes to the impact it will have on our employees.

"Our short run solution is to establish a norm for executives where they ask the managers first to take the potential assignment and work out a plan containing several elements. One element is to create a clear statement of what they are to accomplish, and what things are outside their scope of responsibility. A second element is to define at least two alternative approaches to address the assignment: one focusing on the most important objectives with the least impact on resources and other activities going on in the group; the other detailing a more thorough approach that requires higher effort and cost. The third element of the plan would be optional. After discussing the first two elements with the executive, the manager may raise concerns about the value of the assignment to the organization and what unintended negative or positive impact it might have on other parts of the organization. The manager may then suggest other creative ways to meet the underlying need. Even at our table, we have often seen major changes that require a lot of effort, but are so complex that the end result is far short of what was expected. What we need are some bold managers who will suggest that we try something simpler first and get that to work before we move on to the more complex outcomes. Let's actually use the 80-20 rule. Let's do a pilot with a subset of the organization or a particular department that really wants to change. Let's not be held hostage to the idealists that insist on doing something just because it's possible and sounds good, especially if the benefits are not substantial and quantifiable."

As the Accounting Director is speaking, he is reinforced by nods and verbal confirmations from others in the room. Feeling even bolder, he goes on to the table's long term solution. He says, "Where staffing levels allow it, encourage managers to designate certain experienced individuals to be available for periodic projects. These are generalists who can work with other departments, who know how to tap the resources of the department for specific knowledge, who can recognize potential problem areas, and, above all, who can push back if necessary on well-meaning but costly schemes like those we have been discussing. These generalists can free up the managers, supervisors, and workers to keep on doing their jobs. Of course, the issue is that no one can spare such people because they have regular duties. The challenge is to create job descriptions that carve out from other positions the ad hoc, periodic, and non-critical activities that may be high value, but are not tied to everyday production or customer demands. These might involve analysis, troubleshooting, documentation, project management, and so forth."

I thank the Accounting Director for his contribution and ask for another table to summarize the results of their discussion.

A seasoned Director of Product Engineering rises and says that his table took a very different approach. "We figured that others would tackle the issue of how to reduce stress on individuals being asked by their managers to do too much over a long time period. We appreciate that solutions such as the one just suggested are needed; however, the deeper issue is how to get managers, as well as their employees, to recognize when stress is becoming unhealthy, and how to handle it in a healthy way."

"We feel there are several signs that stress is becoming unhealthy. Here are three. One is an increased or more frequent lack of trust, either in leadership, in your employee, or in your colleague. This leads to unproductive defensiveness, procrastination, or backbiting when asked to do something by someone you don't trust. Conversely, if a manager doesn't trust her employees in a certain area, she will excessively micromanage and criticize their work."

He continues, "A second source of stress is fear, which can take on many forms, such as fear of the future, fear of failure, fear of others' opinions, or fear of change. While some fear can be healthy, it often gets out of control and becomes a major source of stress. We will spend inordinate amounts of energy to try to avoid or alleviate things we fear might happen, only to find that they rarely do come about. This unnecessary activity is a major source of stress.

"A third source of stress is anger, or in extreme cases, rage. Again, while some anger can be healthy, most of the time it is a major cause of stress. This stress is experienced not only by the object of the anger, but also, and more insidiously, by the one who is angry. This is especially true when someone cannot control their anger.

 "We also agreed that these issues of mistrust, fear, anger, and others, don't just harm work relationships and affect our productivity and creativity, but they are also at the root of problems at home. We seem to be able to put on our best face at work, but at home we let down our guard and tend to let these things control our emotions and relationships much more easily. This is especially true with our spouse and children. The things we couldn't express at work boil over into criticism, manipulation, and other forms of subtle, or not so subtle, abuse. Of course, this contributes to the vicious cycle of taking home problems to work, and then the escalating work problems affecting our home life, and so on."

It is at this point in our discussion that someone at another table innocently says, "Aren't these things we call causes of stress actually symptoms themselves? I mean, the question is why do we mistrust, why are we fearful, and why do we get angry and hold grudges? If we are going to deal with root causes, what is causing these behaviors?"

This takes us all by surprise. The Director of Product

Engineering, who has remained standing, senses the quiet tension in the room and says, "OK, you have an excellent point. There probably are deeper root causes. Sounds like that could get more into psychology, though. Reminds me of a Dr. Phil episode a couple of weeks ago on how issues from childhood affect how we interact with people every day. I'm sure we wouldn't want to go there in a business environment."

He paused to allow some nervous laughter in the room to die down. "But," he continues with a slight smile, "if our Owner has made developing and enhancing relationships such a priority, and stress is caused by malfunctions in those relationships (my engineering term), perhaps it is worth some attention. It would fit in well with the other kinds of wellness support that we receive. I don't have any good ideas on what that might look like, but I know that there is a significant cost for operating out of mistrust, fear, and anger as we saw discussed in the video clip."

With that, he tosses the ball back to me. As the HR VP, I'm supposed to be the expert at all things warm and fuzzy, like interpersonal relationships. But I don't have a good answer off the top of my head. Frankly, I have not seen much of this type of training be very effective. It's often superficial, which doesn't tend to be long lasting enough, or it is very intensive therapy, with a high price tag and a huge investment of time.

So I smile at the group and thank the Director of Product Engineering's table for their very creative and insightful results. I say that defining the issue, the real root cause, as they have tried to do, is the most important step in finding solutions to problems. I tell them that I will take their perspective, as well as those of the other tables, into account as I formulate a plan for reducing stress and improving relationships throughout the organization.

Enhancing Relationships

I have trouble sleeping that night, thinking about the results of the exercise with the executives. I don't know what I was expecting, but I certainly am at a loss as to what to do about the relationship issue. I decide that, instead of worrying about it, I'll discuss it the next day with the Owner. I owe him a status report on the project he gave me, so perhaps he will have some ideas. After all, he is the big proponent of healthy relationships as a foundation to success.

I mention this to my wife at breakfast, and she encourages me to take the recommendations of the table seriously, even the idea of how childhood issues can affect relationships today. She agrees that it is not a likely topic for the typical organization to tackle, but then we aren't a typical organization.

In my meeting with the Owner, I have a number of topics for his consideration, a couple of high-level decisions to make, and then a quick recap of the session using the video clip to stimulate discussion. A little bit unsure of myself, I inform him of the first table's thoughts. He nods approvingly and even adds a few ideas. He suggests forming a cross-departmental team made up of experienced generalists that would meet quarterly to discuss proposed studies and other projects that were submitted to them. They could put together a process for initiating and dealing with these issues so that proposals brought to them would be well thought-out and could be reviewed by an executive team to determine priorities. The other benefit, he suggests, would be to formalize these newly created positions throughout the organization so that directors would want to have good people on the team to represent their departments. I tell him I will draft a proposed charter for the team and will present it at the next executive meeting.

I then, almost apologetically, summarize the other table's recommendations to implement a program designed to improve relationships at the personal and family level as a way of addressing strained relationships in the organization. I don't go into much detail, because I don't have a good solution, and I'm not convinced he is going to want me to spend much time on this one. I am quite surprised by his immediate interest and enthusiasm. He wants me to go into more detail about what the people at the table said and how the others in the room responded. After listening for a while, he shares that he has been thinking along these lines for some time. He has seen his theme on improving relationships really help to release cooperation, creativity, and synergy throughout the organization; however, he has also felt, like the second table, that there is more to the story. He has noticed that, even as people are more successful when communication barriers come down, he still senses deeper issues of trust and genuine caring for one another are not being addressed. Results seem to be more task-based, but not person-based as he had hoped. Success in one area doesn't translate into other areas. It takes constant effort to get people to overcome their natural tendency to prefer to work independently or in small groups that build walls.

The Owner pauses, looks cheerfully at me, and says that he wants me to look into programs that might address the personal relationship issue in an organizational setting. He says that he has seen a lot of programs about working with people based on personality types, about teambuilding, and so forth, but he is concerned that these don't go deep enough into the types of long term issues raised by the employees at the table. He has a feeling that there are such programs out there, but traditional corporate providers may not offer them. Such programs may be seen as being too personal and intrusive, or involving long-term therapy. He says, however, he is not afraid to try something new, even if it's on an experimental or pilot basis. I agree to do some preliminary research and report back to him any examples of different programs that might fit our needs. He asks me first to develop some criteria to help screen such programs, and to get input from those who attended the session.

I am skeptical about this whole idea, of course, but in deference to the Owner, I follow through with the research. I first visit with the Director of Product Engineering to brainstorm some preliminary criteria so I will have something to pass on to the rest of those who attended the session. We both feel unqualified to do this, but after a couple of false starts, we develop some key points. We decide that this program should be able to work with large numbers of people at a time, while also being able to focus on individuals and their one-on-one relationships with others. We also want something that could be done either in short sessions over a period of time, or over one or two days in a retreat setting. That should narrow the candidates significantly.

We also want the program to deal with the real root issues of relationship problems. We don't have any preconceived ideas about what that means, but we want some confidence that people would experience real change at the gut level. We aren't interested in techniques on how to control behavior, but we also know that the Owner is going to expect real, lasting results. Finally, and probably the most challenging, is confidentiality. The process has to encourage honesty and yet maintain utmost confidentiality if there is group interaction. We both agree that these are good starting points for criteria, but we also agree that finding programs that meet all of these criteria is going to be difficult.

I call the original group together for a quick debriefing on what the Owner has asked us to do, and I hand out the criteria that the Director of Product Engineering and I have created. I ask them if they have questions about what we are looking for, and I ask them to give me their feedback within a week. One of the sales executives asks if we can have a quick brainstorming session now. I wasn't expecting that, but since he is an experienced and unassuming leader, I ask him to facilitate. He jumps up and begins immediately to solicit ideas by asking the group what is one question they would have for a potential provider of such a program.

A number of responses come in rapid-fire order. They include predictable questions such as who developed the program and what are their credentials, what other organizations have used this and were they able to quantify the results, how long have they been doing this, and how many have gone through it? But then we get some unexpected ones, such as can spouses and other family members be included, and would you be willing to take a group of executives through the program as a proof of concept? Those last two questions illustrate to me that people know they have issues with relationships at a deep level and really want to do something about it.

Over the next week, I get some helpful feedback from the executives, and I meet again with the Owner to summarize the results and discuss next steps. He surprises me by latching on to the suggestion about a group of executives being the pilot. He says he wants to be a part of it, not just to set an example, but for his own sake. He confides he has always had issues with his stepson and he hopes this might help. Nothing else has, he says sadly. He also likes the idea of providing the program to family members. He says it would be like a family health plan, and the organization might even want to subsidize part of it if it turns out to be effective with the employees. I am blown away by his unqualified acceptance of a concept that seems to be very idealistic, especially since I've never heard about a program that meets even part of the criteria we have established, much less seen something like that implemented. I am caught between the enthusiasm of the Owner, and my own skepticism at being able to find anything close to what he is expecting.

Selecting a Relationship Program

My nationwide search has uncovered several programs that, surprisingly, seem to meet some of the criteria, so I form a team to evaluate them. I select the team along the lines of the interdepartmental problem-solving model that was suggested. We first review their materials, have some phone calls with the principals, and check out their references. We decide to bring in three of the firms for the final face-to-face evaluation. Again, the Owner surprises me by wanting to participate in the final evaluations. He suggests that we ask each to spend a full day with us. He wants them to spend no more than an hour of introduction and review of their program, materials, personnel, and pricing. He then wants the rest of the day to consist of a mini-version of their program for the evaluation team. He says that he hopes to get results for the evaluation team members, not just see a demonstration of the program. The final decision will be based on the degree to which the process impacts the team members on a personal level. Again, I am not just surprised, but dumbfounded at my boss. I knew he subscribed to this whole concept, but this shows me just how serious he is.

When I present the three firms with the requirements, two of them immediately agree and schedule dates. The other firm is reluctant, saying that this doesn't fit their methodology very well. They typically don't see results for several months, or even years, because we are dealing with very deep personal issues and people don't change quickly. I politely inform them that we will call them later if the other candidates don't meet our expectations; however, I realize that the length of time it takes for people to see personal change should be another criteria we need to evaluate. We hadn't thought of that one, but a program that could get genuine results in a relatively short time would be an obvious winner.

The First Candidate

I am totally consumed with fear. It's the day for the first vendor to take some of the executive volunteers through their relationship enhancement program, as they call it. It's normally a two-day retreat, but they have streamlined it per our requirements. They feel that it can still be successful since we have a fairly homogeneous group, and their Facilitator can assume certain levels of understanding and motivation to ensure solid participation. We meet in one of the new conference rooms with lots of A/V capabilities and configurable furniture, which allows them to seat us at tables that are nearly round. They explain that this will make group activities more effective. The variable white noise also helps to ensure confidentiality, since participants cannot tell what is being said at the other tables.

The Facilitator explains that the purpose of the day's activities is to engage both our minds and our hearts in experiencing ways to deepen our relationships with others. He says that the main result will be the ability to trust others at a gut level. They have found this is a key obstacle in interpersonal relationships of all kinds, especially in teams who must come together for short periods of time to work on important projects. Our day is to be made up of short video clips that illustrate an issue, followed by a facilitated discussion with the entire group, and then confidential table talk to apply it to our own situations. The videos are really well done and enable the group to address each topic enthusiastically. The topics include how we unconsciously evaluate someone in the first few minutes, how past relationships affect how we form new relationships, and how to understand and deal with difficult people.

The first two topics address barriers we put up that prevent us from having a healthy relationship with someone based on a realistic assessment of their contributions to a joint goal. Many in the group are surprised at how easily they form negative and wrong opinions of others, to their own detriment. The third topic is a bit more controversial. The table discussions are quite animated as executives with different backgrounds and personality types have very strong opinions about how to deal with others who exhibit negative characteristics. We discuss those who constantly dominate the conversation, those who are eternally pessimistic or unrealistically optimistic, those who are distracted or don't want to participate in a meaningful way, and so forth.

As we get past the initial impulse to work around or ignore these different personality types, the Facilitator brings us back to applying the lessons from the first two topics. We begin to see that, while most difficult people have issues of their own, as do we, the real issue is our recognition of how we are putting up barriers that push them away and prevent us from being able to trust them to contribute anything of value. We stereotype people quickly, and then we react to that stereotype as we have been programmed through many past experiences.

For example, if someone talks loudly and fast, we quickly fear that they are going to try to dominate the discussion. Then, based on past dealings, we either confront them, perhaps politely, perhaps not so politely, with the intent of curbing their personality, or we take the opposite approach and constantly defer to them, figuring it is a lost cause to even try to change their style. Either of these approaches, however, plays to our preconceived stereotypes and keeps us from being genuine with that person. That leads to a lack of trust, and as a result, we get little benefit from the relationship. If anything, we become more resistant to engaging with that person in the future.

A better approach is to suspend judgment based on their style, and instead focus on their words. Perhaps they do have something of value to say. We may just need to put up with their loud and fast-paced speech pattern. It may be that they are feeling insecure or uneasy in a new situation and speak this way as a nervous reaction. Or they may have been the youngest in a large family and developed the habit to get attention. In any event, instead of evaluating them so quickly, we need to be aware of our initial reaction and evaluate how our response may be contributing to a lack of meaningful communication.

As we look at this simple example of the underlying basics of relationships, we learn a series of related principles. We should first look for evidence of our own shortcomings and prejudices, then work quickly to overcome that knee-jerk reaction. Next, we should try to assume the best about the other person, not trying to read too much into their words or body language. If we don't work through these steps, without even realizing it, we are likely to bring in a lot of our own baggage and to inflate our own tendency to be critical. Better to give them the benefit of the doubt, withhold any thoughts of criticism, look for as much value as we can find, and then reinforce what good we do see in them.

"But," one of the participants asks, "what if you keep trying to find the best in someone, but over time they prove themselves to be superficial, unreliable, or just plain malicious? How can you have a healthy relationship then?" The Facilitator smiles, as if he has been waiting for a segue, and gives the group a scenario and asks a question. "Imagine a relative who, after all these years, still bugs you. You have every reason to want to be friendly and accommodating, but things they do and say make it impossible. You want to ignore or not be around them at all, but you don't have any choice since they are part of your family. What do you do?" As people immediately raise their hands to tell about their worst relative nightmare, he laughs and asks us to turn back to our tables to discuss this with real life examples.

One table gets very loud, so the Facilitator turns the white noise up a couple of notches. Everyone is animated about this topic. After some time, he asks for volunteers to report their suggestions, without going into details about specific relatives, of course. One of the marketing directors offers to give three bullet points from her table. "First," she says, "the longer you know someone, the harder it is to change your opinions and attitudes towards them. So, in the spirit of looking at yourself first for the solution to relationship issues, we suggest that, instead of retreating from such difficulties, or worse, attacking them, we thoughtfully engage them on their terms. It may take swallowing our pride, but perhaps we can find some common ground that will avoid the hot buttons that set them off. For example, if they constantly harp on politics, we could steer the conversation to their favorite football team or a recent movie they saw. We should really listen and learn from what they have to say, asking probing questions to draw out their knowledge and feelings about the less controversial subject. We might be surprised at how much we can learn from them, or that we actually have areas of agreement that can lead to a more positive relationship. But it takes sacrifice on our part to reach out to them and find such areas of communication."

The table's second bullet point involves listening. They suggest that it is not just about active listening that focuses on what the other person is saying rather than on what you are going to say next, but it is really understanding what they are saying and what underlying motivation or deeper issue might be behind their words. The Marketing Director says, "A common example is the person who is constantly negative and critical towards someone else or about a particular topic. It might be a boss or an associate who has let them down, to the point that they have lost trust in that person and constantly belittle them. Or it might be a product that has problems, such as software or a new piece of equipment the organization has started using. Our suggestion is to listen carefully so that you can restate the issue in a sympathetic, but clear and objective manner. Then listen again to how they react. If they ignore your attempts to identify the problem and discuss solutions, but keep harping on how frustrated or distrustful they feel, there may be something else that is triggering their reaction. We suggest that perhaps they are under a lot of stress from unrelated issues and this is just a convenient opportunity to vent. Or perhaps the current situation evokes a similar past problem that didn't have a good ending, and they are fearful that the same thing is going to happen again. Or maybe they may have a legitimate complaint, but no one else is listening and they are frustrated that nothing is being done about it. As you ask helpful questions, or make sympathetic statements to better discern what is really going on, you can try to help them discover the root cause. That won't solve the problem, but clarifying it can lead to a more constructive dialog."

The table's final bullet point is counter-intuitive and takes the whole room by surprise. The Marketing Director lowers her voice for contrast, and says, "Our final suggestion is to disengage completely from a person who doesn't want to behave differently after you've exhausted all of your best efforts to engage them and listen to their real issues. At some point, it may be better both for you and for them to keep a polite, but firm, distance. Even with relatives, you can be at the same function, but you don't have to listen one more time to their rants, boasts, or tales of self-pity. Of course, it might be a bit more difficult if the person is your boss or an associate you work with every day, but the same principle applies. You do have to watch out for your own attitude toward them. Again, in the spirit of looking towards your own feelings first, you do not want to become frustrated or bitter. That will only hurt you and others around you. Nor do you want to be unrealistic and pretend everything is fine, insincerely flattering the other person to mask your true feelings. The genuine approach is to be patient and wait for opportunities to make small improvements in the relationship. Perhaps you can recognize a minor accomplishment at work or in their off-duty activities. At some point, they may experience a crisis with which you can help. In the meantime, you are better off not feeding their frustrations or criticizing them behind their back. It will reflect badly on you, and will not be a useful foundation from which to ever reconcile the relationship."

The Facilitator wraps up the day's activities by summarizing the major points brought out by the discussion times, and adds a few of his own. He emphasizes the primary principles that you are only responsible for your own attitude, and that it is generally not helpful to try to change others on your timeframe. "People can change," he says, "but it is usually driven by events in their lives and internal motivation, not by well-meaning critiques, however constructive. Our main goal in having healthy relationships is to maintain a positive attitude, and have patience with others. We should assume the best about others' intentions until proven otherwise, and listen to what they are really saying that reveals their underlying feelings. They may not even be aware of how their actions and words are driven by deep-seated feelings that come from past experiences. As careful listeners, we can discern when there is more than the obvious at work. We can be careful not to make matters worse by trying to fix the superficial problem, which can trigger even deeper reactions."

I thank the Facilitator, his organization, and everyone in attendance. I ask them to complete a quick survey that has just been emailed to their smartphones. The purpose of the survey is to evaluate how they feel the day's activities have changed their attitudes towards others, and how they think it might help them improve their existing relationships and form new healthy ones. I encourage them to put the principles they have learned into action over the next several days, and alert them that in two weeks they will receive another survey to see if they have made progress in that short time period. Their frank answers will help us determine how we will select and design a program that can be used throughout the organization.

The Owner catches me after the others have left and asks what I think about the first program. I respond that it was good and makes me think about how I react to people and situations without really listening and assessing what is happening at a deeper level. I am not sure if I can operate in that mode day after day, but I can certainly see the benefits of trying. The Owner agrees, and adds that he was impressed with the emphasis on looking inward for things you can change in yourself to help improve relationships. It is always good to focus on self-critique before critiquing others.

He asks what the next step is, and I say that the second program is being presented next week to a different group of executives. I ask if he is planning to attend it as well. He smiles and says to try to keep him away. He is very intrigued at the possibility of having a significant impact on his personal attitudes towards others, as well as gaining insight in how to help others overcome relational barriers. He is more convinced than ever that this can make a huge difference, and that it may be able to release the organization to work together with new levels of creativity and positive energy.

As I reflect on the day's results and the Owner's comments, I am actually starting to get excited about the prospects of offering such a program in the firm. This was just a taste of what can be done, and I can see where follow-up sessions and offerings to employee families could be of great value. Besides the impact on relationships in the workplace, I think it would send a strong message to the employees that the firm really cares about them as individuals and wants to see them healthy and productive in every aspect of their lives. It almost sounds corny, like the old days when most people expected to stay with an organization for their entire career. I know those days are gone forever, but maybe we can help people maximize their potential while they are with us. That has to translate into better results for the organization in the short run, and perhaps it will do so in the long run as well.

The Second Candidate

I am almost reluctant to confirm arrangements for the other program. But as I look into it from the perspective of the first program, I realize that it may go even deeper into identifying and dealing with the source of relationship problems. It promises to look into hurts from the distant past that never were resolved. It starts from the premise that these relational wounds cause us to damage important present-day relationships without knowing why it is happening. Sounds like the Dr. Phil personal psychological stuff to me, but I'm hooked on seeing how this might apply in the workplace. I am surprised at the positive feedback already coming in from the first program, so I'm ready to try anything that might help our people enhance relationships and trust.

The Facilitator arrives in the same conference room, arranged in the same way as for the first program, but he asks that the table groups be mixed up so people who work together are not at the same table, and so the men and women are separated. He explains that he wants to establish a high degree of confidentiality, and asks for agreement to not disclose any personal responses beyond the people at the table. Also, he has seen that people may be hesitant to talk freely if there are others present with whom they work and whom they know well. Any mention of confidentiality gets the attention of my HR ears. These are seasoned executives who are going to know their boundaries in a group setting, so I am not too worried – yet.

The Facilitator gives an overview of the program, which is aimed at identifying the symptoms of broken relationships in our lives, discovering and dealing with the root cause of the problems, and then restoring the relationships that have been broken. I can sense the eyes rolling and hear the nervous shuffling as he adds that often the root cause is an offense we suffered as a young child that can be attributed to something one of our parents either did to us, or failed to do. Just when I am wondering how that could affect what's happening in my life today, he asks us to close our eyes and think about the earliest childhood memory we have of a serious pain that we felt involving the action, or lack of action, by one of our parents, or someone else who was responsible for our care at the time. I reluctantly close my eyes and try to think of something. It took a bit, but finally I am remembering going to kindergarten for the first time in a city we had just moved to, and I was deathly afraid of going in to the school building by myself.

Just as I was starting to relive the experience and feel some of the fear from what happened later that day, I notice a man at the table next to me reaching for a tissue. He has his back to me, but as he uses the tissue to dry his eyes, I realize it is the Owner! Something has obviously caused him to feel strong emotion, so I don't feel quite so awkward about my own reaction to a distant childhood incident. A couple minutes later, the Facilitator asks us to take some time at each table and, if we feel comfortable, and without a lot of detail, tell the group what came to mind and how it made us feel. I am curious what the Owner is saying at his table, but I can't hear because of the white noise and the fact that the other tables are talking in animated, but controlled, tones.

I mention to my group the kindergarten incident and the bullying that took place later that day. I hadn't thought of that story in a long time, but it still brings up such unpleasant memories that I notice my voice filling with emotion and my fist clenching. I describe my mother's insistence that I be a big boy and go into the school building by myself, and how my dad dismissed my angst when I shared the bullying incident with him later that evening. I feel my jaw tensing up and my face getting flushed. I am surprised at the level of emotion, but it passes as the next person tells his story. I am amazed at the impact this simple exercise is having on these seasoned professionals. It is obvious that most have deep-seated feelings about past offenses that still can stir up emotional responses.

As the day progresses, we learn about the kinds of negative behaviors that come from various types of early offenses, and the resulting fear, bitterness, and anxiety that dogs us the rest of our lives. As with the first program, I see that the focus of this one is also on us as individuals, and about dealing with our response to problems instead of responding to other people's behavior. I even bring this up at one point in the session, and the Facilitator simply says that our ability to get free of the controlling negative forces, such as bitterness, is not dependent on the person who is the object of our bitterness. They may never admit their offenses, much less ask us to forgive them. They may even be dead.

He said it's like being mugged and stabbed while walking late at night, and insisting that the ambulance wait on taking you to the emergency room until the mugger is caught and is forced to apologize to you. The bitterness you have towards your offender might be justified in your mind, but it doesn't hurt that person, it hurts you. He says the Chinese have a proverb about bitterness – it is like drinking poison and expecting the other person to die. I don't consider myself to be a bitter person, but I do recognize that I have, and have had all my life, a rather distant relationship with my parents. I never quite seem to trust that they have my best interests at heart. I am beginning to wonder if something like the early kindergarten incident could be a contributing factor, or even a root cause for that broken relationship.

The rest of the group seems to be very engaged in the remainder of the program that day. We do several exercises to describe painful incidents in our lives, and even write letters to forgive those who hurt us. I have to admit I feel very relieved, after all these years, to clear the air about how my dad's handling of my being bullied really made me feel. I see how I began to not trust those in authority, and instead learned to watch out for myself.

As an adult, I took it a step further and became determined to control my environment as much as possible so I wouldn't allow anybody else to bully me or to disappoint me when I was hurt. Once, I even shut my wife out from helping me work through a serious relationship issue with one of my bosses. It became so severe that it threatened our marriage for a time. So in the final exercise, I write a letter to my wife admitting how I have shut her out from key aspects of my life, preferring to handle these things on my own, and ask her to forgive me for not allowing her to help me through the tough times. I can't believe how light this revelation makes me feel. I can't wait to get home and talk to my wife about it.

On the way to my office, the Owner catches up with me and is eager to talk about the day. I wasn't planning to embarrass him by asking about the tissue episode at the beginning of the day, but he brings it up right away. He says that when he closed his eyes, he was immediately a four-year-old, huddling in the dark in his bedroom listening to his father yelling at his mom and threatening to hit her for something she had bought. While his dad regularly targeted his mom, he was also the brunt of the man's anger from time to time. He was always afraid of his father and never had interaction with him, other than being severely evaluated for everything from his schoolwork and sports to his dating choices as a teen. He moved out of the house as soon as he could, and determined that he would do everything possible to be kind to his wife, family, and everyone around him.

These feelings, suppressed for many years, all came back in rapid succession as he closed his eyes. He said he couldn't control the tears as he felt the fear, anxiety, anger, and determination to separate from his father. Later in the day, he realized that he also blamed his mother for defending his father and not taking steps to protect herself or him. He was then able to see how that led to his desire to create safe, perfect environments for himself, his family, and the organizations he eventually led. In the process, however, he drove himself hard to prove that he was worth something. He now realizes he has been trying to prove himself to his father, and deep down there are resentments about the sacrifices he has had to make. His drivenness has also caused his employees to work long hours and often neglect their families.

He says that writing the letters was the hardest, but most liberating thing he has ever done. He chose to write a letter to his employees, recognizing the harm he has imposed on them because of his perfectionism and culture of overwork, and then apologizing and committing to doing better. He is beginning to see that perhaps his emphasis on relationships, while good in itself, may have been born out of guilt for expecting so much and looking for ways to get even more out of his people. He reads me his letter, which almost brings tears to his eyes. I am flabbergasted when he casually says he intends to send it in the first class mail to every employee at his or her home address. He wants to make sure each employee's family reads it, and that they all have the opportunity to forgive him for the harm he has caused. I start to dissuade him from such a rash and risk-filled action, asking him to wait for a few days to make sure. He agrees to do so, but I can tell his mind is made up.

He then confides that the real revelation from the day is the harm he has done to his stepson. He realizes he has taken much of his suppressed anger out on the boy, just as his father did to him. He is ashamed of what he has done, and he is going to write a letter and share it with his stepson tonight. As I commend him for this, and turn to leave him with his thoughts, he directs me to a simple desk plaque on a bookshelf, almost in the shadows. He wistfully asks me to read it out loud. It says, "He will turn the hearts of the fathers to their children, and the hearts of the children to their fathers." I ask him what the phrase "Malachi 4:6" at the bottom of the plaque means. He says it's from the last verse in the Old Testament. A rabbi friend had given it to him years ago, and every now and then he reads it for encouragement when he has a blow-up with his stepson. He says that now he knows how that verse can happen. I nod, and once again turn to leave, this time with a tear in my eye.

PART THREE – The Community

I am the Mayor. The tower Owner is my new friend, and we have worked together well during the search for the location, construction, and occupancy of the tower. My City Manager has more direct contact with the Owner and his people, and she speaks highly of him and the entire organization. My relationship with the Owner was cordial to begin with, but it continued to deepen into respect, even admiration, as we dealt with building codes, environmental regulations, zoning regulations, and issues with nearby businesses. The tower is obviously a great economic boon to our city, but we are also amazed at the energy and resources the organization is putting into the community. Besides the normal response to calls for help with charitable projects, they are actually using their business skills to help us improve our municipal services and plan for growth.

It started with the initial phase of the building project. We had very clear guidelines for the organization to determine the impact of their proposed tower on the infrastructure, traffic, noise levels, and pollution in the area. The Owner not only agreed with all of our requirements, but he also hired a well-known municipal Planning Consultant to suggest other ways the project could help improve those areas, as well as the surrounding businesses and neighborhoods.

The City Manager worked directly with the Planning Consultant to identify how nearby businesses could complement the Owner's organization. In one case, a well-established, local maintenance and janitorial service was given a long-term contract with up-front funding to help expand their staff and to implement a high-quality training program for existing and new employees. They were also able to invest in the latest equipment and upgrade their supplies. A competitor across town cried foul, and the Planning Consultant suggested that they work together. The first company found that the competitor had specialized expertise in state-of-the-art HVAC systems, and subcontracted all of that work to them. The competitor was pleased, since this was their most profitable line of service.

The Planning Consultant also worked with the public transit system to make minor adjustments that would provide the maintenance and janitorial workers with convenient schedules during the non-peak hours when they were coming on and off duty. Another example of improving municipal infrastructure involved upgrading the traffic flow and parking around the tower area. The Owner funded an in-depth study to identify improvements that would not only accommodate the additional employees, but also take into account the likely growth in surrounding businesses and residential housing.

The Owner was particularly interested in promoting multi-family housing and recreational areas that would be attractive to the employees. He even worked with us to obtain tax credits that would be designated for employee housing subsidies in the nearby complexes. He made the very convincing argument that the reduction in traffic and parking needs would offset some of the infrastructure impact. It was a unique win-win situation that was written up in a national urban planning publication, and eventually won a prestigious award for the City Manager.

The most unusual impact the organization continues to have on the city, however, is not related to the government. The Owner sponsors a task force of his managers and senior employees who have a variety of entrepreneurial skill sets. They are reaching out to small businesses in the area and are providing one-on-one coaching in areas such as marketing, sales, customer service, and financial analysis. The goal is to help them expand their businesses for the economic benefit of the city as a whole, but especially to create an atmosphere of excellence and a commitment to help one another as they are being helped. This latter benefit was a bit unexpected, and is mushrooming beyond even the Owner's expectations.

The degree of willingness to help one another with business problems is unlike anything I have ever seen. The civic organizations still work formally to help charities and bring more business to the city, but they spend most of their informal conversation during the regular meetings asking for, and giving, help to one another. Examples include loaning specialized equipment to help a neighboring business when they have machine breakdowns, raising money to help a struggling new business meet their insurance deductible after a devastating fire, and holding roundtables to learn about one another's businesses so they can refer customers. They've even brought in a customer service training program for multiple downtown businesses that will provide visitors to the city with a consistently excellent experience, from taxicabs and restaurants to nearby shopping and entertainment venues.

The Park Incident

There is one area, however, where the tower received some negative publicity. The park area underneath and around the tower at ground level recently appeared to be a victim of its own popularity. Many of the employees use the child care facility in the tower, and the playground area is always full of energetic preschoolers. Everything was going well until passersby also began to enjoy the park. While the playground is separated from the rest of the park with an eight-foot see-through fence, anyone can come up to the fence and spend as much time as they want observing the children. Parents in the tower do so frequently on their breaks; however, a few parents began to notice someone seeming to take an unusual interest in the children. Upon approaching him, the parent would find that the person looked confused and quickly walked away. After several complaints, the tower Owner hired an additional policeman to patrol the grounds, regularly touring the park and the playground area. He has instructions to ask non-employee loiterers to move on, which is difficult to do since the park is advertised as being open to the public.

Of course, the city has the same problem with loiterers in many areas of downtown, especially around municipal buildings and parks. The difference is the playground in the tower park has observant parents nearby. A couple of the more vocal parents are not satisfied with the patrol and are asking for security cameras with internet access. While the park is private property, the tower Owner sees it as a community resource and is reluctant to agree to their request, especially since most parents do not seem to be concerned. The vocal parents, however, come to a city council meeting and request that the city require prominent security cameras with real-time internet access covering playgrounds that have public access, whether on private property or not.

As chair of the council, I ask them what evidence they have that there is really a problem. They show a phone video of a disheveled man leaning up against the playground fence, making funny faces at one of the children. The police officer comes by and asks the man to move. When the man hesitates, the officer takes him by the arm and unceremoniously escorts him out of the park. The couple smile as they stop the video projection on the chamber screen and claim that this incident shows the dangerous behavior that needs to be discouraged with prominent cameras throughout the park.

As I am about to thank them for their concern and ask for the next petitioner, a well-known homeless activist strides angrily to the microphone and complains that the video clearly shows excessive force being used by the police officer. He requests that the petitioners provide a copy of the video, which they do, and then the activist stuns the audience with the story of the man in the video who is supposed to be a threat. He is a long-time homeless man who is deaf and spends his days going from one busy location to another, entertaining passersby with a simple, humorous mime act. He especially likes to do it for children. He is mentally challenged and rarely gets in trouble. Many people give him donations, although he doesn't solicit them.

I seem to remember a newspaper article a couple of years ago about the man, similar to what the activist was describing, so I quickly thank him and the petitioners for their input and try to move on to the next petitioner. However, by now, two or three reporters are crowding around the microphone, taking pictures and asking questions. The petitioning couple are confused about all of the attention, and still don't realize that their concern about the children is being pre-empted by the tower policeman's rough handling of the homeless man. In vain I try to maintain order, but by now the activist realizes the opportunity to raise old grievances about the city's handling of the homeless population.

The next morning, the headline in the Metro section of the newspaper features the incident with a picture from the video. The full video is in the online version of the newspaper and is being picked up by several other news and social media sites. This is looking like a major negative publicity event, and the newspaper is stoking it by starting a series on the homeless situation in the downtown area, which they clearly had in the files and were waiting for the right time to publish.

I suspend my schedule and call a meeting with several department heads and the Director of Communications to determine what we can do to handle the spate of publicity. There is a lot of hand-wringing from the group about how much we do for the homeless and how the media is not being fair. While I agree, I also know that it has been a while since this topic has had any top-level attention, so I challenge the group to look for a way to turn this into a positive opportunity. After a more wandering but lively discussion, I finally end the meeting and resolve to get the tower Owner involved. He started this, and dodged a bullet at my expense, so he owes me one. Surprisingly, I get right through to him and he agrees to meet me for lunch. I pick a diner on the outskirts of the city to avoid more attention. Our conversation over hamburgers is animated and draws the attention of the server, who recognizes me and quickly figures out who the Owner is. She asks if she can interrupt to make a comment. We both smile, and I reluctantly say, "Of course."

The server, of all people, happened to be watching the council meeting on television last night. She had turned accidentally to the broadcast while making an evening snack. She says she was fascinated by the unexpected drama in the usually boring session. She tells us that she had a dream that night about the homeless man in the video. He was doing his mime act in a different park, and several giggling children and their parents had gathered to watch him. Then, she says, in her dream she saw him afterwards walk away from the park through a series of streets and alleys where he finally came to a large crate that was obviously his home. He lay down inside it for an afternoon nap, but first drew out a photograph wedged between the slats. She saw two children in the dog-eared, faded photo. They had big smiles and had an arm around one another, making a funny face at whoever was taking the picture. The homeless man sighed and brought the picture up to his lips. She could tell that he was mouthing the words, "My darlings." He finally wiped some moisture from his eyes, put the picture back in the crack, and lay down for a nap. We wait for her to continue, but she pauses, says, "That's all," and turns around to wait on a customer who had just sat in the booth across from us.

Problem Solving

We stare at each other for a minute, and finally I say that we have got to do something. This is not right that people like that are living on the streets in our city. The Owner agrees, and we begin to discuss earnestly what can be done. I start by recounting both the history and the current state of the homeless, including assistance provided by the city, non-profits, and private companies. As I tell the story, I realize that, while everyone involved has had good motives, and a lot of tax dollars and charitable contributions have been expended, the end result has been disappointing.

The Owner takes it all in with uncharacteristic silence. He finally asks a simple question. What is the root cause of homelessness? I protest that there is no single cause, but in reality, there are many – lack of education and job skills, physical and mental disabilities, drug addiction, chronic depression, and emotional trauma, to name just a few. I add that we have a variety of programs that attempt to address these issues. The Owner persists, however, in asking for the root cause. While initially I am at a loss, I quickly see that he is not expecting me to have the answer.

He continues to probe and says, "When we have serious and complex problems in my organization, we pull together those who are affected to better define the symptoms and the overall impact. We usually reduce them to costs. The costs we're analyzing don't end with our bottom line, but include the cost to the customer, to our employees personally, to opportunities forgone by our stockholders, and even the cost to the community, both locally and at large. Once we put a dollar figure on these impacts, they become much more real and help us see the big picture.

"When this happens, we typically find that it is easier to define what we call the 'cost drivers'. These become the focus of our problem solving, and as we analyze them further, we almost always find a small set of root causes. Often there is a primary root cause, but you are right that it is not always that simple. The key is to look at the problem with as large a perspective as possible, and not restrict it to what we may think is only within our scope of responsibility. Looking at the issue that way would make it easier to define and solve as a simpler problem, but it doesn't usually touch the root causes, and because of that, the symptoms are only partially or temporarily alleviated.

"For example," he continues, "when we built the tower, we looked at the effects of our decisions as broadly as possible, even to the point of assigning dollars to the emotional and physical costs of moving our employees' families here from all over the country. It made us realize the gravity and magnitude of what we were about to do, and prompted us to take extraordinary measures to alleviate those costs. We did this not only with traditional monetary assistance, but also with other programs, such as counseling services for the children being uprooted from their schools and friends."

"I don't see where you are going with this," I interrupt. "How does this apply to the homeless problem?"

The Owner takes out his tablet and says, "Let's estimate the costs of homelessness, not just to city services, but to the homeless person, his family, the business and property owners in the area, and even those who are walking by who may feel uncomfortable with his behavior."

As we do this odd exercise, I begin to see the magnitude of the problem, especially when multiplied by the hundreds of homeless people in our city.

We continue down this train of thought and begin to name the root causes. I have a lot of experience and knowledge on this topic, so we quickly narrow the category to just three main ones. The most obvious is lack of a job and the income to pay for housing of any kind; however, that leads to why they can't get and keep a job. There are two main reasons – first, physical disability or addictions, and second, mental and emotional dysfunction. The Owner argues that it is the latter that is the root cause, with emphasis on the emotional side. I agree that while there are fine government and private programs that help people recover from addictions and provide meaningful work for the physically and mentally limited, those who are not emotionally stable are often not able to stay in these programs, or do not even want to try.

He then asks me, "What do you think is the issue with the homeless man in my park?"

I refer to the server's dream, and say, "It may be that he has had an emotional trauma involving loss of his children. His deafness can be overcome, but if his heart is broken, he may have given up on providing for himself. Perhaps all he cares about is trying in some small way to establish connections with other children to replace what he has lost."

The Owner stares at his plate for a long time. Then he tells me about the program that his HR Vice President brought into the organization and the impact it has had on the employees and their families.

"It is all about restoring broken relationships," he says. "You would be amazed at how many issues, even health related, are connected to long-standing relationship dysfunction. The most amazing thing," he continues, "is that with a little teaching and guidance, people can often find a root cause in their childhood that continues to affect their emotional health today."

I am a little skeptical about mixing work and emotional health, but I see the connection with the homeless situation. I ask him, "Do you think something like that might help the chronic homeless?"

The Owner smiles and says, "I will have my HR VP meet with you and others you select to review what has happened in our organization. Then you can judge for yourselves. Be sure to include one or two homeless, or ex-homeless people."

I tell him I will definitely take him up on his offer. As I am driving away from the diner, my mind is racing with ideas on who to invite and what this could mean to our city's homeless program. I am sure he is oversimplifying the problem and the potential solution. At the same time, I have to admit that most dramatic television series and movies I've seen recently have a father or mother relationship problem at the root of someone's dysfunctional behavior. I can see how my folks' divorce when I was six years old has affected me. How much more would the terrible childhood situations of many of the homeless affect their emotional and mental stability?

It may be messy, but I am determined to take the next step and see if there is anything the city can do to bring some light to this dark and seemingly hopeless condition.

The New Tenants

Five years have passed since the opening of the tower, and I have a dilemma. The Owner just informed me that his organization sold off a major division as part of their long-term consolidation strategy, and almost a fourth of the tower will be leased out to other occupants. I am sad because of the loss of the employees, many of whom have played vital roles in the community, but at the same time hopeful because of the quality of companies that will undoubtedly be attracted to this prime space. The Owner assures me that he will partner with our regional development council to give priority to businesses that will most benefit the city's overall economic and cultural health.

I suppose I should be surprised that he approached me about this rather than the other way around, but I have come to expect the unexpected with him. He also surprises everyone by announcing that the organization will be reshuffling floors to occupy the lower three-fourths of the tower, leaving the prime top floors for new occupants. He confides to me that this is not primarily an economic decision, but that he believes his organization will benefit by having the best possible tenants sharing the building and being a part of the community.

As the word spreads about the available space, my office is flooded with inquiries from prestigious firms regarding city services, development plans, and tax considerations. As part of the tenant application and evaluation process, the Owner has assembled a diverse team, including several representing other businesses and governmental bodies, to interview the candidates and provide analyses and recommendations. I've never seen anything like it. You would think he's assessing candidates for acquisition rather than mere building tenants.

High on the preliminary evaluation list are two large international law firms expanding their offices to include our city. I question the Owner about continuing to consider both firms, thinking that he would not want competing firms. He says competition is not only healthy, but in his experience it is essential for achieving excellence. He also has noticed that most firms, even large ones, tend to have a few specialty areas. He suspects that two such firms will have opportunities to complement one another or supplement one another's resources. And of course, they would both use similar support staff and services, so a larger pool of such resources would benefit both of them. Once again I am amazed, if somewhat skeptical, at his counterintuitive approach to bringing people and organizations together. He always seems to find a way to promote cooperation, even in the midst of fierce competition.

Sure enough, the two law firms are both selected as tenants, occupying most of the vacant space. Several smaller professional services firms make up the rest. It is an interesting mix, but each occupant has definite opportunities to benefit from working with the others, including, of course, the Owner's organization. They all sign long-term leases, and settle into the space. Several of the firms knew about the architectural and interior design innovations but are not prepared to take full advantage of them. The Owner is eager to help, and forms a transition team, comprised of his own managers, to offer mentoring and training in the use of the building's unique facilities and furnishings. The transition team understands that change does not just happen through orientation and training classes, so they arrange to meet monthly for the first year. They also offer to come to the new tenants' offices to observe meetings and everyday activities, with the purpose of making suggestions for further use of the special capabilities. For example, the variable white noise generation in every room is completely unfamiliar, and the meeting facilitators require several reminders before they begin to take advantage of the privacy and calming effect produced.

While assisting others in how they could better use the building features, the team realizes their own organization could use some periodic reminders. They even learn a few tricks from some of the more creative tenants; for example, how to tune the white noise in individual offices to complement the occupant's work style. I have plans to refurbish one of our older city government buildings, and I am eager to see if we can include some of these innovations.

The Owner and His People

One of the first things I noticed about the Owner of the tower, when I met him many years ago, was his affable nature and charm. After having been around him and his associates a lot, I now see where it comes from. He is careful to encourage and compliment his people in front of others, and they in turn do the same thing for their people. The whole organization is friendly and easy to work with. People are not stressed out, and take a genuine interest in what you have to say. They even probe beneath the surface to find out the real cause of any issues, which invariably makes it easier to resolve them. I think this atmosphere of cooperation and concern for others feeds on itself. Most are confident and at ease with themselves, which in turn makes them at ease with other people, and so forth. It's just a fun group of people to be around.

But don't get me wrong, they are not pushovers, nor are they idealistic. Like the Owner, his people value truth, they do everything they can to get the relevant information about an issue, and they look at issues from all perspectives. This, I believe, is what gives them the confidence to know they are doing the right thing, and enables them to not to have to resort to bullying or other tactics to get what they want. As an example of the atmosphere that permeates the organization, I heard a report recently of one of his managers bad-mouthing the city government during a break at a city-sponsored function. Within the hour, the manager comes back to each person in the group and apologizes for his words and attitude. It turns out two of his colleagues cornered him privately and counseled him on his behavior. They said it reflected badly not only on the organization, but on him as a part of the respected management team. They did not tell him how to fix it, but he knew immediately that he had to make it right with everyone who had heard his public complaints. My staff is still talking about the incident.

The Commission Hearing

As the Mayor, I am participating in a planning and zoning commission hearing this week, which involves potential widening and re-signaling several streets around the tower. The whole area has grown dramatically, and traffic problems have accompanied the growth. The open hearings are to review the in-depth traffic, environmental, and economic impact studies that we commissioned almost a year ago. As expected, the Owner offered to include some of his specialists on the study teams at no charge to the city, so he is already quite familiar with the findings. He is curious, however, about the feedback from other businesses and residents in the area, so he gives me a heads-up that he is attending the hearings himself. I would normally be suspicious of a top executive wanting to sit through such hearings, but now I understand that he is simply expanding his understanding of how the surrounding businesses think. He always wants to know how others perceive a particular issue, especially when it has an impact on his organization.

As the hearings get started, he is on the second row, inconspicuously taking notes on his tablet computer. At the conclusion of the first day, I invite him to have a quick bite so that I have a chance to hear what he is learning and thinking about the study results.

He begins by thanking me for allowing his organization and him to be involved in the studies. I tell him that we are glad to have the expertise. I relate the commissioners' comments that the loaned specialists were very helpful and did not seem to have an agenda. In fact, one of them uncovered a significant problem with a proposed freeway ramp change that would have marred an iconic view of the city that has almost become a trademark. Another of his specialists realized that the traffic studies revised the one-way street patterns in a way that was less favorable for the tower occupants as they were leaving the building during rush hour; however, the overall flow in the city would be improved. The specialist agreed that this was the ultimate objective of the study, regardless of the impact on his fellow employees and tenants. He then devised a plan for the tower to rearrange its parking garage flow to work better with the potential change in the adjacent street patterns. He also included a recommendation that the organization expand its flex-time policy to allow for a wider variation in employee arrival and departure times. He made the study team feel that the change could actually turn out to be a benefit for the organization instead of a negative.

Then I say to the Owner, "But of course you know all of this, don't you?" He smiles and admits that he has biweekly briefings with the specialists that have been loaned to the city commission. I suspect that he has had more influence on their actions than anyone realizes. I turn the conversation to the hearings. He says that he has learned a lot about how the other businesses perceive the city planners and is surprised that they seem to be defensive about every recommendation. It seems as if they're looking for how the changes might have a negative impact on their businesses, rather than how the recommendations might benefit the city as a whole, especially the improved traffic flows for their potential customers and suppliers during non-rush hours. Citing the example of his organization being willing to change its parking and flex-time arrangements, he says that other businesses may have similar opportunities to adjust to the proposed changes that would actually help them. They just need to take the time to explore their options.

I had noticed the same reaction from the business owners who asked questions and commented on the study results at the first day of the hearing. But it is a normal occurrence at these types of hearings, so I didn't think much about it. Such hearings are typically a debate to see which side has the better arguments based on facts and analyses. Our goal at this point is to win the overall case, not to address every minor objection in detail. Sure, we could probably find creative solutions like the tower Owner's organization did, but that requires a lot of effort and cooperation from the many businesses involved. It would undoubtedly extend the time and cost of such changes.

When I verbalize my thoughts to the tower Owner, he gives me his signature knowing smile, and suggests that in future studies like this, the city might consider creating more opportunities for earlier involvement by those impacted. He further suggests offering workshops to stimulate understanding of the overall objectives and to help business leaders see options they might have to use potential changes for their benefit. He says he would be happy to have any of his specialists speak at, or even conduct, such workshops, using their experience as an example. Once again, I am amazed by his willingness to sacrifice his resources for the benefit of the larger community. As if reading my mind, he says, "You know, we always get more out of these efforts than we put in. It may take a while, but the attitude of helping others gets returned many times over when we need help or when we need consideration from others on changes that impact us." I can't argue in his case, since the organization is successful financially and by any other measure.

As the second and final day of hearings comes to a close, I am surprised when the tower Owner asks to speak. He doesn't have a question, but rather faces the audience and commends those gathered for being active in the community and involved in important decisions that affect city infrastructure. He also commends the commission and other city officials in the room for the transparency with which they have conducted the studies and this hearing. He says that his organization fully supports the recommendations that have been proposed and amended during the session, and he hopes that the others in the room will do the same.

He acknowledges that not every detail of the proposal is what he would have chosen, but now he understands better the variety of competing interests. He sees that it is necessary for all parties to give up a little convenience and to bear some additional costs to achieve a better overall solution, especially for the citizens who work, shop, and visit this area of the city.

"It is our workers and customers who make us successful, and we owe it to them to provide the best experience possible," he concludes. There is a smattering of applause as he sits down, and I can tell that even those who didn't fully appreciate his comments are thinking about what he said. The tower Owner may have been stating the obvious to the city planners, but such thinking is not so obvious to most business owners who have a much more self-centered view of what is good and bad about infrastructure and other governmental changes.

The Law Firm Dilemma

It's a few months later, and I have another unexpected encounter with the tower Owner. The city has solicited work on a number of related matters from several local law firms, and it just so happens that the two firms in the tower have been selected for different pieces of the work. There is one area, however, where we are asking them to cooperate, since they have different areas of local expertise that are needed on one matter. Of course, both firms are telling us that they can handle the matter themselves, and that there is no need to involve the other firm. Their solutions, however, involve using attorneys from other offices who have the requisite expertise. That is exactly what we want to avoid since the case is very sensitive and involves a dispute between members of a prominent long-term city family who have expressed their preference to use specific attorneys with whom they have relationships. The attorneys just happen to work for these two different firms.

The City Attorney and I meet with the local office managing partners of the two firms separately and hear each one's adamant refusal to work with the other firm. Of course, the fees are substantial, but I sense there is more than just revenue at stake. I ask each managing partner in turn if they would be willing to contact their counterpart to discuss the issue, and in both cases their body language as well as their words left no uncertainty as to their feelings about the other person. I can easily see that this is not just about economics, or even pride in their firms. It is clearly personal.

The City Attorney and I discuss our next step after the meetings and decide to ask the tower Owner to intervene. The firms are his tenants, he has great people skills, and we think he might enjoy a challenge of this type. One of the attorneys even lives in a luxury condo near the top of the tower and plays handball with the Owner in the tower's health club. However, when we present the background of the work and the current dilemma, he surprises us again by asking to not be involved. As we press him for a reason, he finally confides that he has been aware for some time of the deep-seated issues between the two office managing partners. It came up when they both held discussions on moving to the tower space, and it was made clear to the Owner that, while the firms could coexist in the same location, they were serious competitors. In fact, they required certain privacy concessions, such as separate elevator banks, so that client confidential conversations would not be overheard.

The Owner thought it was a bit odd that the two leaders never agreed to be in the same meeting. Other firm attorneys and administrative personnel did not seem to have that issue, but the two leaders definitely kept their distance. The tower Owner also suspected that there were personal issues at stake, and without revealing the specifics, he confirmed that it was not difficult to find out from public internet sources what those issues were. As a result, he is very reluctant to get involved in their interpersonal affairs.

Having served four terms as mayor, I do not get discouraged with people who initially turn down my requests for help, so I persist. I plead with him on behalf of the prominent family, whom he has come to know quite well. I also appeal to his reputation as a complex problem solver and an expert in interpersonal relationships. I ask him to consider the scenario where he transfers in an executive from another office and later discovers that the executive has a conflict with an executive with whom he now has to work. Would he ignore that situation? That catches him off guard, and he finally says he will get back to me. Of course, the next day he calls and says he will attempt to resolve the issue on my behalf, but is not hopeful. His attitude of pessimism is very uncharacteristic, so I consider my expectations managed.

Relationship Resolution

A week later, the tower Owner calls and says he has good news and bad news. I ask for the good news first, trying not to get my hopes up. He says the firms will work together on the matter as we are asking them to do. I am in shock, but take a deep breath and ask for the bad news. I hear a chuckle on the other end, and he says, "The bad news is that it is going to cost you a very expensive dinner to find out how it happened."

I know he is kidding about the expensive dinner, but I gladly call his bluff and arrange for dinner that night at the best restaurant in town. After we order, he quickly, almost excitedly, tells me the story. He says that he decided to get the two in a room and simply confront the underlying issue that made it impossible for them to communicate with one another. He describes a consulting technique he learned many years ago called "name the resistance." He continues in his best mentoring tone, "When you suspect that you will encounter resistance to a proposal, you simply bring it out into the open as part of stating the proposal, and deal with it in explicit terms. For example, if the service you are pitching is expensive and you suspect your customer is in a budget crunch, you lay out the truth so they don't have to force you to go there. You then show how the benefits will more than offset the costs, even in the short run. If you dance around the underlying issue, it gives them the opportunity to politely resist your position. They may not even tell you the real reason, if it puts them in a negative light. However, stating truth is always a powerful tool, especially if you then combine it with another technique, which is to draw them in with questions. Making assertions tends to put people on the defensive, whereas asking questions tends to draw them toward you, since they are the ones now making the statement. Of course, you lose control when you ask questions, but that's the power of it. It's counterintuitive, like 'the meek shall inherit the earth' and 'pride comes before a fall'. People grudgingly acknowledge that there are lots of examples of these ancient truths, but rarely do they believe it in the daily stress of life. No, you have to stand up for yourself, because no one else will. Anything perceived as weakness is shunned. And so forth."

As the Owner continues with the story, he says he called the two attorneys into his office, ostensibly to discuss a facilities issue. He arranges three chairs in the center of his office so they would all be facing one another with nothing in between. When each realizes that the other is also in the meeting, they immediately protest. The Owner asks them, "Don't you want to know why I have taken this huge risk to call you both in at the same time?" They freeze, and slowly sit down, not wanting to make a scene in this respected man's office, but also wondering what he could possibly be up to.

Taking their response as permission to proceed, he says matter-of-factly, "I have looked on the internet at your mutual histories and the controversy in your former law firm, and I believe I understand why you parted ways a few years ago; however, I don't understand how that alone would explain the gut level reaction you have to one another just being in the same room. I do have a facilities issue to discuss that affects your firms, but the real reason I called you in at the same time is to see what's behind this refusal to work together on a high-profile case that will benefit both firms. It's even come to the attention of the Mayor, for goodness' sake, and he asked me to intervene. It's really none of my business, but for the reputation of your firm, and as a fellow business executive, landlord, and I hope, your friend, I ask you both, what is really behind this destructive reaction?"

The tower Owner pauses, takes a long drink of iced tea, and continues the story. "The first office leader clears his throat and starts to protest, but he quickly admits that I am right. He has not been able to work with the other attorney since the incident at their former firm. He starts to explain what happened, but the other office leader interrupts him, claiming, 'That's not what I intended at all. I was just trying to help an important client and keep the firm out of trouble.' The first office leader raises his voice, and I can tell that a shouting match is about to start.

"I stop them with a simple request. I ask each to describe, in three or four sentences, 'What were your motives in taking the actions that you did during that controversy? Not the actions you took, but how you were really feeling during that time and why you were doing what you did. And don't be self-serving or polite. I want the real gut-level story. What was going on inside you?' They both got quiet and finally the second office leader told how he was feeling about what happened, and why he felt he had to take the actions he did. It took him a little over two minutes. Then the other did the same thing. After about thirty seconds of silence, they both began to say things like, 'I didn't realize you felt that way, I thought it was all about the money,' and, 'I had no idea the client was putting that kind of pressure on you,' and, 'Why didn't you say something at the time?'"

The appetizers arrive, and as we are admiring the presentation and flavors, the Owner gets back to the story. He says, "I see that there has been a typical miscommunication, but it almost seems ludicrous that it could have caused the palpable tension that was in the room just a few minutes ago. So I ask them one more question, 'How in the world did this misunderstanding mushroom into such a chasm in your relationship? You are two brilliant, successful attorneys. You make a lot of money helping other brilliant, successful people come together for billion-dollar deals. What is going on here?'

"They both pause for a long time. It is creepy to have so much silence with two high-powered attorneys in the room. The first finally admits, 'You know, I guess I just couldn't handle the attitude. Most of us thought of one another as family, but when things fell apart, he came across as defensive, accusatory, and blaming me for what went wrong. I see now that isn't what he was thinking at the time, but it just rang my bell.'

"So I ask them, 'Why do you think you were so sensitive about this? I have been through some things in the past few years that showed me how hurts I had in my childhood caused behaviors in later life that I have come to regret. My father was never satisfied with my performance, so I became a driven perfectionist to show that I deserved what he was never able to give me, which was affirmation of my worth as a person and a professional. Only recently have I begun to understand and connect the dots to my adult behavior patterns. Is it possible your over-reaction and resulting long-term grudge was somehow rooted in such a childhood hurt?'

"'I hadn't considered that,' said the attorney, 'but I guess it did remind me of how my father would rant and rail at me when I didn't perform on the field the way he thought I should, even though he would never help me and missed most of my games. He always made excuses, but now that I think about it, his anger toward me was probably his way of deflecting his own shame at not being there for me and being responsible for my failures. I don't know, maybe his father treated him the same way. I'm sure I'm overthinking this, but I don't know why else I would have pulled away from my colleague here when he needed support from the firm. That's what I would do with my dad. Rather than try to find a way to help him, I would withdraw to keep from being hurt even more. I doubt I could have helped him, even if I had wanted to. But now I know I do want to repair this relationship today.' He offers his hand to the other attorney, and says he is sorry for his anger and resentment over the years. As they shake, the other says he is sorry as well for jumping to conclusions without having all of the facts. While he was surprised that his colleague might have been implicated in the wrongdoing, he admits he was jealous for the firm's reputation and probably struck out prematurely. He also takes responsibility for the rift between them. He says he does not do well when anyone pulls away. He assumes, as he did in this case, that the other person is to blame, and basically writes them off. Following the other attorney's frank disclosure, he likewise says he probably picked up this behavior from his childhood as well. When his parents divorced and his mom left the family, he hadn't seen her since, and has no desire to."

As we begin to work on our salads, the Owner ends the story at this point, saying that the men seemed to be reconciled, and at least agreed to each work on the matter using the attorneys requested by the family.

I thank him, and say that he definitely earned the dinner.

He isn't finished, however. He says that the incident has reminded him that he has a similar issue himself. As part of the relationship reconciliation program in his organization, he was able to make peace with his stepson, but he never took steps to reconcile with his father. He says that if these two elite attorneys can bring themselves to forgive one another and recognize that their long-standing feud stems from their broken relationships with their parents, the least he can do is try to approach his father about the past.

I am uncomfortable saying anything that isn't complete support, but I have to admit that I really don't get it. In the spirit of being honest, I ask him if he's sure he wants to open an old wound that maybe his father doesn't even understand or think is relevant this many years later. What if he makes things worse by bringing it up?

The Owner pauses to think about this as the entrees arrive. He finally looks me in the eye and says, "This is not for my father, it's for me. I have to know that I've forgiven him for how he treated me, but it has to be real. He has to understand that it hurt me, and I have to know that I've tried to make it right. Even if he blows it off or tries to make excuses, I have to do this. There is too much at stake. I love the man in spite of everything. He's my father, and I owe it to him to try."

At this, I realize I am in over my head. I've obviously struck a deep nerve, and I don't know what else to say. As we continue to carve up our steaks, we make small talk, but there has been a major deepening of our relationship, just in the process of talking about such things.

After ordering dessert, the Owner excuses himself to go to the men's room. My thoughts wander back to my childhood. I can't think of anything that caused bad feelings, so I guess I am pretty lucky. When the Owner returns, I say that it must be difficult to talk about the past like that, and I mention that I can't really see anything in my past that caused hurt. "My dad was a model father," I say. "He loved my mother, provided for us kids with a great job, and he was and still is well respected in the community and church. I just don't have any negative memories of him or my mother at all."

The Owner says, "You are truly lucky. You know, the Facilitator in our organization's relationship program said there are two kinds of hurts from the past. He identified the aggressive ones, usually abuse of some kind, whether physical, verbal, or emotional. Those are easy to identify, like mine was. However, the other kind of hurt, the passive ones, are not so obvious.

These are where we didn't get something from one or both of our parents that we should have. We may not even realize it. For example, maybe the father was loving and kind, but he was preoccupied with work and often wasn't able to be around for our school or sports events. Or maybe the parents divorced quietly, without a big fuss, and he just became a small part of our life, not intentionally hurting us, but not being there when we needed him to be."

"Now that you mention it," I say slowly, "my father was away on business a lot. He traveled all over the world and brought us back awesome presents. We went on amazing family vacations using the frequent flyer miles he accumulated. But he wasn't there much the rest of the time. I never thought about that being a negative, but I guess he did miss a lot of my games. He even missed award banquets, like the one where I was named the athlete of the year. I was really proud, and my mother made a big fuss and put the trophy on the fireplace mantel. But my dad was in Europe and forgot to ask about it when he called the next day. I'll never forget how crushed I was. He made up for it later, of course, but I suppose I never really forgave him for not being there on my big night."

I expect the Owner to say something to cheer me up, but he is strangely quiet. He just looks straight at me for a few uncomfortable seconds, and finally says, "I am so sorry." He reaches out his hand and puts it on my shoulder as he says those words. I am actually starting to feel something deep inside my chest. I quickly turn my eyes away, but I can tell that something has happened. I have to find out what this means.

Epilogue

This little book is a series of related parables. While the overarching theme is the value of interpersonal relationships, other moral and business principles are embedded in the stories, such as creativity, honesty, forgiveness, process improvement, consulting, systems thinking, teamwork, and project management. Many of the business principles are drawn from my work experiences and training. Most of the examples of creativity, such as the design of the building and furnishings, are a bit fanciful, but they illustrate that creativity allows out-of-the-box thinking, and doesn't initially have to be practical. The key is to provide an atmosphere for creative ideas, and then find creative ways to implement them.

All of these principles are facilitated and enhanced by improving and maintaining relationships. It is only when we have healthy interpersonal relationships that we can be released to fulfill the creative genius and other moral principles that are a part of our human makeup. Broken relationships are accompanied by fear, insecurity, unforgiveness, pride, criticism, and other negative thinking and emotions that bind us up and prevent us from loving others and loving ourselves. If we can't love ourselves, we can't fulfill our destiny and become who we are created to be.

I, and members of my family, have begun to experience the

restoration of healthy relationships, largely through processes similar to those described in Part Two. You can find out more about our experiences in a book my son, Ben Watts, has written titled "Turning the Hearts of the Fathers," available on Amazon.com. More of our individual stories are included on our website at restoringthegenerations.com. The program we have embraced was developed by Christian psychologist Dominic Herbst. You can find out more about it at restoringrelationships.org. Another resource for the program is Philip Fortenberry's Ministry of Reconciliation Encounters at sacornerstone.org/reconciliation.

My wife, Kathy, and I have used the program in a couple of churches to help hundreds of people. Many come to the classes and encounters because they know they have issues with their spouse, children, parents, bosses, and co-workers. What they don't know is that their current issues are almost always rooted in emotional wounds that occurred in their childhood. As with many similar programs, this one takes them on a journey of self-discovery to identify what happened, leads them to understand how that is still affecting them today, and then helps them work through a process of admission, grieving, and forgiveness that releases them from their bondage to unforgiveness and anger. The intriguing aspect, as illustrated in this book, is that the wound and the resulting effects can be subtle, suppressed, and hard to recognize. It has been amazing to see the light dawn on most people who go through this process, and to watch them receive healing from years of hurts they have experienced, and then subsequently passed on to their family and others.

While this book does not use Christian themes or language explicitly, it was through my personal faith that I felt compelled to write about my experiences as a parable on relationships. I was surprised that the result was secular in nature and included a lot of my personal business background and interests of a non-religious nature. However, since our Creator is by definition infinitely creative, and in my opinion non-religious, I suppose I shouldn't find it surprising that He would lead me in such a direction. I trust, therefore, that non-Christians will find these simple stories and principles intriguing, even counterintuitive, and desire to look deeper into the spiritual reality behind them. I trust that Christians will find the practical applications of these principles engaging, will desire to look deep within themselves for signs of relationship issues, and will seek similar Christian programs that will bring restoration and health.